Andover

A338

Stockbridge

Kings Worthy

New Alresford **9**

Salisbury

Winchester **2** A31

WINCHESTER & SALISBURY

Mottisfont

M3 Twyford

Warnford

Alton

Petersfield

Romsey

Eastleigh

Bishop's Waltham

PORTSMOUTH & SOUTHEAST COAST **8**

Fritham **3**

Southampton

Hamble-le-Rice M27 **7**

Fareham

Waterlooville

Havant

Chichester

2

NEW FOREST

Lyndhurst

Hythe

Fawley

Beaulieu

4 Bank

Burley

1

New Milton

Lymington

Gosport

Portsmouth

Bognor Regis

Christchurch

Milford on Sea

Yarmouth

Cowes **3**

A3054 Newport

Ryde

The Needles

6 Freshwater

Isle of Wight

Foreland

ISLE OF WIGHT

A3055

Shanklin

St Catherine's Point

6 Walk start point

1 Cycle start point

2 Tour start point

ISLE OF WIGHT

Alum Bay ■ Carisbrooke ■ Cowes
Freshwater Bay ■ Godshill ■ Osborne House
Ryde ■ Sandown & Shanklin ■ The Needles

PORTSMOUTH & SOUTHEAST COAST

Fareham ■ The Hamble ■ Hayling Island
Porchester Castle ■ Portsmouth
Southampton ■ Southsea

WINCHESTER & SALISBURY

Alresford ■ Chawton ■ Far
Hillier Gardens ■
Salisbury ■ Sha

D0240717

CONTENTS

Welcome to the...

New Forest
& Isle of Wight

This beautiful region includes some of the best of rural Hampshire, Wiltshire and Dorset, with many of the South's prettiest villages and most appealing small towns thrown in for good measure. It takes in some of its biggest conurbations, too – sprawling cities such as Southampton, Portsmouth and Bournemouth, with historic hearts of gold.

As an area to explore, it simply has to include the Isle of Wight, which remains an entire world of its own, slightly apart from the 21st century. The New Forest, famed for its wildlife conservation and natural beauty, is one of Britain's newest national parks, a status that helps to preserve ancient traditions of land management, and has meant better access than ever for walkers and cyclists. And it would be absurd not to venture along the coast to the chalky Jurassic cliffs of east Dorset, celebrated as a World Heritage

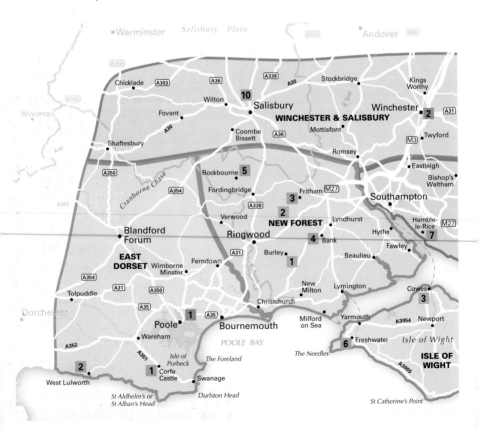

Site. Inland there are the winding streams of rural Hampshire to discover, and historic Winchester with its squat, medieval cathedral and Jane Austen links. From here, cross into Wiltshire to the busy market town of Salisbury, with its soaring Gothic cathedral, or to link the two at Romsey, where a massive Norman abbey completes the trio of architectural gems.

If you enjoy stately homes and museums, some of the best in the South are here, including the National Motor Museum at Beaulieu, the Historic Ships collection at Portsmouth, and grand mansions such as Wilton House, Kingston Lacey, Osborne, and the famous gardens of Exbury and Mottisfont Abbey. There are glorious, golden sandy beaches at Studland, Swanage and Bournemouth, and inland the superb downs, ancient woodland and open heath to discover. There is something for everyone in this diverse region.

6 Walk start point
1 Cycle start point
2 Tour start point

ESSENTIAL SIGHTS

If you have little time and you want to sample the essence of the New Forest and this area: Picnic under a canvas of ancient oaks deep in the forest...join the boating fraternity and sail out of Lymington...visit atmospheric Osborne House...clamber aboard and imagine life on Nelson's flagship HMS *Victory*...dance the night away in the many bars and clubs of trendy Bournemouth...sunbathe on Studland's beautiful sandy beach...walk among the eerie jagged ruins of Corfe Castle...enjoy a gentle train ride on busy Alresford's Watercress Line...listen to the choir sing and admire the stained-glass windows in Winchester Cathedral.

5

1 Lulworth Cove/ Durdle Door

Crescent shaped Lulworth Cove is a popular spot for holiday-makers. Its towering limestone cliffs hold the secrets of its history – fossils that tell of a time when dinosaurs wandered the earth, and before, when this part of the south coast was deep under the sea.

2 Spinnaker Tower

Portsmouth's Spinnaker Tower was the city's main millennium project. It is the city's main tourist attraction and stands 558 feet (170m) high and the viewing platform at the top can be reached by a choice of high-speed or panoramic lifts.

3 Sandown

Since the Victorian era, this gently shelving beach on the Isle of Wight has been popular with holiday-makers and families.

4 Calshot

Colourful, traditional seaside huts are a sign of a long-established beach and this is true of Calshot. It is mostly pebbly underfoot.

5 The Needles

These limestone stacks have long been a welcome sight for weary sailors but many ships have foundered on these dangerous rocks.

6

6 New Forest Ponies
These friendly ponies have roamed free on their ancient homeland of heath and woods for centuries.

7 Shanklin Chine
A chine is a deep ravine, formed here as water has carved out a narrow path through the stone below. The waterfall is a feature of this lovely area that is known for its variety of wildlife and range of flora.

8 Christchurch
The Avon and the Stour meet at this popular town. The riverfront is dominated by moored craft of varying sizes and condition and there is invariably someone painting or renovating their boat moored here. The river itself is always busy with pleasure craft on tours of the area, and Christchurch Priory is not to be missed.

7

8

9

9 Studland

Long and sandy South Beach, Studland, stretches back to hilly dunes and heathland – a national nature reserve – good for interesting treks. The more northern end of the beach is used by naturists. If you are approaching Studland from Poole, take the ferry for a short journey across the Poole Harbour.

10 HMS *Warrior*

Launched in 1860, HMS *Warrior* was one of the fastest vessels of its day, powered by both steam and sail. *Warrior's* gleaming decks can be seen in Portsmouth's Historic Dockyard.

10

DAY ONE

For many people, a weekend break or a long weekend is a popular way of spending their leisure time. These four pages offer a loosely planned itinerary designed to ensure that you make the most of your time, whatever the weather, and see and enjoy the best the area has to offer.

Friday Night

Spoil yourself with an overnight stay at the Rhinefield House Hotel, which lies off the A35 southwest of Lyndhurst. It's a Victorian pastiche of a grand Elizabethan mansion, set in several acres of lovely landscaped Italian-style grounds. Relax in the opulent lounge before entering the grand dining hall for dinner – the menu shows French influence, and there's an extensive wine list.

Saturday Morning

After a satisfying breakfast, head into the popular and busy town of Lyndhurst, the so-called 'capital' of the New Forest. Call in at the tourist office beside the main car park and select your area for a morning's walk, or hire a bicycle and follow one of the many waymarked routes. It's by far the best way to see the Forest up close. Don't forget to call in at the Serpentarium, for a sighting of this region's more unusual reptiles.

Saturday Lunch

After your morning's exertions, pick a good country pub for lunch. You're almost spoiled for choice in this region, but the Royal Oak at Fritham offers a special sort of rural simplicity, and the Trusty Servant at Minstead is always popular, offering a wide range of snacks and full meals.

Saturday Afternoon

After lunch, head west along any of the main routes (the A31–A348–A3049 is probably the least congested), and turn off the A35 at Lytchett Minster for the Isle of Purbeck. Head south, via old Wareham, then pick up the minor road, the B3070, heading down past Lulworth Castle and through Lulworth village to the almost perfect circle of Lulworth Bay. It is worth calling in to the visitor centre here for information about the local geology and fossils, before heading off on a bracing stroll along the cliff path. If it's at all damp underfoot it can be extremely slippery, and walking boots are recommended.

Saturday Night

As evening settles in, meander through the narrow, winding country lanes to Corfe Castle and beautiful Studland, with its long sandy beach. Cross to Sandbanks on the ferry, and pick out a hotel that most appeals to you – the Harbour Heights, on Haven Road, is a great choice. Refurbished and chic, it offers fabulous sunset views over Poole Harbour from its lovely brasserie terrace, and has a stylish, contemporary menu to match.

CORFE CASTLE

WINCHESTER CATHEDRAL

DAY TWO

Our second and final day starts with a visit to the historic port and university town of Portsmouth, with its longstanding importance to the Royal Navy, before driving inland up to the Test Valley and through the market towns of Romsey and Stockbridge on the way to Winchester. End the weekend in this cathedral town, which has ancient monuments and modern restaurants.

Sunday Morning

After an early breakfast, head northeast from Poole, via Ringwood, on the A31, and follow the M27 east to junction 7. From here, follow the A334 through the attractive old market towns of Botley and Wickham. Head south on the A32, then follow the A27 eastwards through Portchester and follow the tourist signs south to visit the historic ships collection in Portsmouth. It's unmissable, with a guided tour of Lord Nelson's flagship, HMS *Victory*, the highlight. If you can fit it in, the waterborne tour of the harbour, including views of the ultra-modern Spinnaker Tower, is a must.

Sunday Lunch

You could easily spend the whole day in Portsmouth, but if you want to explore the area further then drive back towards Southampton on the A27. Call in at the villages of Hamble or Bursledon for lunch at a traditional waterside pub, and watch the Sunday sailors exercising their craft on the river, ranging from streamlined luxury motor launches to humble dinghies.

Sunday Afternoon

Return to the M27 and head west, soon turning off at Junction 3 to visit ancient Romsey. Stroll around the town centre and explore the historic abbey, then continue northwards up the A3057 to the venerable town of Stockbridge. A fly-fisherman's delight, Stockbridge has the trout-filled River Test running through it. Enjoy a cup of tea here and perhaps some shopping along the high street, before heading east into Winchester on the B3049.

Sunday Night

There's a great choice of eating places in Winchester, as you'll discover on a pleasant stroll around the town centre when most of the visitors have gone for the evening. The elegant Hotel du Vin on Southgate offers cosy, top-notch dining in a friendly setting, and rooms at the back avoid the worst of the town's traffic noise – it's a deservedly popular choice, so book ahead.

Route facts

MINIMUM TIME The time stated for completing each route is the estimated minimum time that a reasonably fit family group of walkers or cyclists would take to complete the circuit. This does not allow for rest or refreshment stops.

OS MAP Each route is shown on a map. However, some detail is lost because of the restrictions imposed by scale, so for this reason, we recommend that you use the maps in conjunction with a more detailed Ordnance Survey map. The relevant map for each walk or cycle ride is listed.

START This indicates the start location and parking area. This is a six-figure grid reference prefixed by two letters showing which 62.5-mile (100km) square of the National Grid it refers to. You'll find more information on grid references on most Ordnance Survey maps.

CYCLE HIRE We list, within reason, the nearest cycle hire shop/centre.

❶ Here we highlight any potential difficulties or dangers along the cycle ride or walk. If a particular route is suitable for older, fitter children we say so here. Also, we give guidelines of a route's suitability for younger children, for example the symbol 8+ indicates that the route can probably be attempted by children aged 8 years and above.

Walks & Cycle Rides

Each walk and cycle ride has a panel giving information for the walker and cyclist, including the distance, terrain, nature of the paths, and where to park your car.

WALKING

All of the walks are suitable for families, but less experienced family groups, especially those with younger children, should try the shorter walks. Route finding is usually straightforward, but the maps are for guidance only and we recommend that you always take the relevant Ordnance Survey map with you.

Risks

Although each walk has been researched with a view to minimising any risks, no walk in the countryside can be considered to be completely free from risk. Walking in the outdoors will always require a degree of common sense and judgement to ensure that it is as safe as possible, especially for young children.

• Be particularly careful on cliff paths and in upland terrain, where the consequences of a slip can be serious.
• Remember to check tidal conditions before walking on the seashore.
• Some sections of route are by, or cross, busy roads.

Remember traffic is a danger even on minor country lanes.
• Be careful around farmyard machinery and livestock.
• Be prepared for the consequences of changes in the weather and check the forecast before you set out.
• Ensure the whole family is properly equipped, wearing suitable clothing and a good pair of boots or sturdy walking shoes. Take waterproof clothing with you and a torch if you are walking in the winter months.
• Remember the weather can change quickly at any time of the year, and in moorland and heathland areas, mist and fog can make route-finding much harder. In summer, take account of the heat and sun by wearing a hat, sunscreen and carrying enough water.
• On walks away from centres of population you should carry a mobile phone, whistle and, if possible, a survival bag. If you do have an accident requiring emergency services, make a note of your position as accurately as possible and dial 999 (112 on a mobile).

CYCLING

In devising the cycle rides in this guide, every effort has been made to use designated cycle paths, or to link them with quiet country lanes and waymarked byways and bridleways. In a few cases, some fairly busy B-roads have been used to join up with quieter routes.

Rules of the road

• Ride in single file on narrow and busy roads.
• Be alert, look and listen for traffic, especially on narrow lanes and blind bends and be extra careful when descending steep hills, as loose gravel or a poor road surface can lead to an accident.
• In wet weather make sure that you keep an appropriate distance between you and other riders.
• Make sure you indicate your intentions clearly.
• Brush up on *The Highway Code* before venturing out onto the road.

Off-road safety code of conduct

• Only ride where you know it is legal to do so. Cyclists are not allowed to cycle on public footpaths (yellow waymarks). The only 'rights of way' open to cyclists are bridleways (blue markers) and unsurfaced tracks, known as byways, which are open to all traffic and waymarked in red.
• Canal tow paths: you need a permit to cycle on some stretches of tow path (www. waterscape.com). Remember that access paths can be steep and slippery so always push your bike under low bridges and by locks.
• Always yield to walkers and horses, giving adequate warning of your approach.
• Don't expect to cycle at high speeds.
• Keep to the main trail to avoid any unnecessary erosion to the area beside the trail and to prevent skidding, especially in wet weather conditions.
• Remember to follow the Country Code.

Preparing your bicycle

Check the wheels, tyres, brakes and cables. Lubricate hubs, pedals, gear mechanisms and cables. Make sure you have a pump, a bell, a rear rack to carry panniers and a set of lights.

Equipment

• A cycling helmet provides essential protection.
• Make sure you are visible to other road users, by wearing light-coloured or luminous clothing in daylight and sashes or reflective strips in failing light and darkness.
• Take extra clothes with you, depending on the season, and a wind/waterproof jacket.
• Carry a basic tool kit, a pump, a strong lock and a first aid kit.
• Always carry enough water for your outing.

Walk Map Legend

⇢	Route	▨ ▨	Built-up Area
❶	Route Waypoint	▨ ▨	Woodland Area
– – – –	Adjoining Path	🚻	Toilet
☀	Viewpoint	P P	Car Park
•	Place of interest	⊟	Picnic Area
⌂	Steep Section	START	Cycle Start Point
⊟	Picnic Area		

East Dorset

The region of eastern Dorset incorporates a variety of pretty, pocket-size villages and towns, and a stretch of coastline that is famous for its fossil cliffs and is dubbed England's Jurassic Coast. With chalky downland, the woodland of Cranborne Chase, the high ridges of the Purbeck Hills and the glorious golden sands of Studland and Bournemouth, there is plenty of variation in the landscape too. Follow in the footsteps of Lawrence of Arabia, Thomas Hardy and the Tolpuddle Martyrs as you explore.

KIMMERIDGE

CORFE CASTLE

LULWORTH COVE

BOURNEMOUTH

Unmissable attractions

Walk along the golden, sandy beaches of Bournemouth or Studland...climb up to the haunting ruins of Corfe Castle...visit the grand 17th-century mansion of Kingston Lacy...marvel at the rock formations in Lulworth Cove and the stone arch of Durdle Door that sits just off its beach...take part in a nostalgic Punch and Judy show while enjoying an ice cream at the Victorian pier at Swanage...act out the part of an army commander and climb aboard an authentic tank at Bovington's fascinating Tank Museum...picnic in the rolling grasslands of Cranborne Chase surrounded by a mist of colourful butterflies...fill up on fish and chips at Poole's thriving quayside.

1 Corfe Castle
The castle was destroyed during the Civil War after a long siege. Then, the defenders were allowed to leave before the castle was damaged beyond repair, in order to prevent its further use.

2 Bournemouth Pier
The pier underwent a costly renovation in the early 1980s and is now an essential attraction along Bournemouth's seafront.

3 Lulworth Cove
Although popular with those who favour paddling and sitting by the sea, the area surrounding Lulworth Cove and Durdle Door is wonderful for anyone who prefers to walk and enjoy the variety of landscape here including open spaces and narrow, chalk paths.

4 Kingston Lacy
The wealthy Bankes family built Kingston Lacy as their new home after their family seat, Corfe Castle, was destroyed in the Civil War. Kingston Lacy has been renovated and houses a renowned collection of paintings.

5 Cranborne Chase
Cranborne Chase is part of the UK's sixth largest Area of Outstanding Natural Beauty and is characterised by gently rolling chalk slopes.

6 Poole
Poole's large natural harbour determined its future as a port, and made it an important centre for boat and yacht building. Poole quay is usually busy with visitors and locals, whereas the old part of the harbour is much quieter.

BOURNEMOUTH MAP REF SZ0991

Bournemouth is the queen of the south coast holiday resorts, with its 6 miles (9.7km) of fine golden sands. In addition it has a pier complete with striped deck chairs and theatre for nostalgic summer shows, orderly winter gardens, palm-tree-lined parks and a compact town centre dedicated to serious shopping, as well as a vast hinterland of suburban sprawl.

Unlike its more serious neighbour, Poole, Bournemouth has never really been anything other than a resort. It was a small village in the early 19th century, at the time when many of the pine trees that now scent the air were first planted. Blessed with a mild climate, and a south-facing location in a sheltered cleft, the settlement boomed towards the end of the 19th century, and most of the town's central buildings date from this period, with Victorian buildings interspersed with some later art deco. New luxury blocks of offices and modern accommodation may have changed the skyline for ever, but the town's heart has a comfortable, old-fashioned feel that still appeals to many holiday-makers.

The town centre is shaped around the Lower, Centre and Upper Gardens, a long, leafy park around the flowing Bourne stream, with magnificent island flowerbeds, scenic tethered balloon flights, an aviary, a mini-golf centre and various refreshment stops. Around the upper end and the Square cluster all the main shopping streets, with arcades leading off the largely pedestrianised Old Christchurch Road. The most appealing of these is the glazed 1866 Victorian Arcade housing the well-known Dingles department store and designer outlets including Gucci and Karen Millen. Beales is Bournemouth's large independent department store. Opposite it is St Peter's Church, with Arts and Crafts wall paintings, a chapel dedicated to the Oxford Movement reformer John Keble, and the grave of novelist Mary Shelley (and the heart of her brother, the Romantic poet) in the churchyard.

The lower end of the park runs past the Pavilion Theatre, under the main road and out onto the seafront, with the pier just ahead. Bournemouth's pier is a functional affair, reinforced with ugly concrete that has seen it survive when others along this coastline have been washed away. Photographs at the far end show how it was partly demolished during the Second World War to prevent its use in a possible German invasion. Now it has a pier theatre and amusements, and great views back to the town, and the western beaches with their beach huts tucked under the sandy cliffs. A land train offers transport up and down the seafront. The twin domes near the pier entrance mark the

■ Insight

BEACH HUTS

These wooden chalets are an integral feature of seaside resorts, and date back to the days when sea-bathers were taken modestly out into the shallows in horse-drawn wooden huts on wheels, before entering the water in full costume. Today they offer a bit of home on the beach, and sell for tens of thousands of pounds. At Bournemouth, however, you can rent them by the day – ask at the tourist office.

aquarium, and the modern glazed building on the seafront is the IMAX cinema complex. Set behind this, on the East Cliff, you will find the interestingly turreted Russell-Cotes Art Gallery and Museum, which is home to a collection of fine Victorian paintings and treasures.

BOVINGTON MAP REF SY8388

The Royal Artillery, the Infantry and the Royal Armoured Corps train their drivers on a £6 million all-weather circuit near Bovington, and there has been military training in the area since the first tanks were introduced during the First World War. Bovington's Tank Museum explains it all, and has the world's largest collection of around 250 armoured fighting vehicles, and exhibits from 25 countries – you don't even have to be a tank fanatic to enjoy it. Mock battles and rides are offered in summer. One corner is devoted to 'Lawrence of Arabia', who has strong links to this part of Dorset.

In nearby Moreton churchyard is a stark slab of white marble inscribed: 'To the dear memory of T E Lawrence, Fellow of All Souls College, Oxford. Born 16 August 1888, died 19 May 1935.'

The brilliant, enigmatic and haunted figure of Lawrence continues to intrigue people. As British liaison officer to the Arab Revolt, Lawrence proved himself a leader with an ambitious personality and an extensive knowledge of strategic warfare. His flamboyant courage and adoption of Arabic dress gave him heroic status as Akaba was captured in 1917, and Damascus achieved in the following year. Lawrence remained involved in Arab affairs even after the war, lobbying

■ Visit

MORETON GLASS

Moreton church was rebuilt after bomb damage in 1940, and its chief delight is its windows. What from outside looks like plain glass, from inside is revealed to be engraved with a vivid flow of delicate pictorial designs. The etching is the work of the late Lawrence Whistler (more of his work can be seen in Salisbury Cathedral). The window (1982) in the Trinity Chapel particularly rewards closer inspection; it is an anonymous memorial to an airman killed over France during the war, and tells of a brief marriage cut short, illustrated by magnolia blossoms, a sunburst, and a crashed biplane.

unsuccessfully for Arab independence. Finding fame a millstone, he joined the ranks of the RAF in 1922, seeking a degree of security and regular life as Aircraftsman Ross.

Discovered, he first enlisted in the Tank Corps at Bovington in 1923 as Private T E Shaw, and moved to Dorset, buying a derelict house at nearby Clouds Hill (now National Trust) as an evening and weekend retreat. Clouds Hill is a bachelor house, with a gramophone, well stocked bookshelves, comfortable firesides and few frills; it became his 'earthly paradise'. Lawrence finished writing his account of the Arab Revolt, *The Seven Pillars of Wisdom* (1926), here, and in 1925 rejoined the RAF.

In 1935 he retired to Clouds Hill, but on 13 May that year, returning home on his Brough Superior SS-100, he swerved to avoid cyclists and was thrown from the motorbike. He died five days later; the legend is still very much alive.

Worth Matravers to Corfe Castle

Worth Matravers is a picturesque village, complete with duck pond. Men from here have worked the nearby quarries for centuries and local stone was used to build Salisbury Cathedral. By contrast, the huge, toothy ruin of Corfe Castle seems to fill the gap in the wall of the Purbeck Hills with its presence. It stands on a high mound, and must have been incredibly imposing when whole.

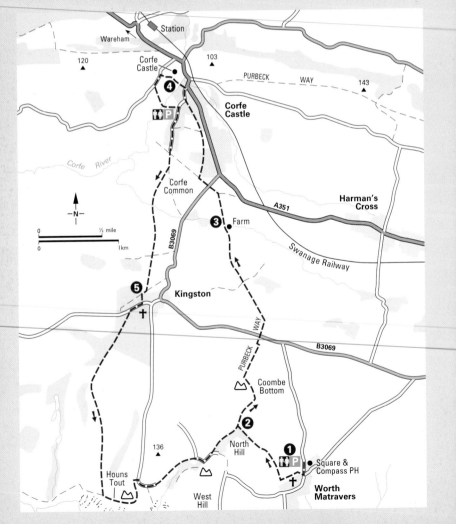

Route Directions

1 Turn right down the street and soon go right, up a path by a fingerpost. Turn left through one gate, then a further two, walking behind the village. Turn right at the end, cross the wall and continue down the next field. At the bottom bear left over the stile, walking down a narrow cutting.

2 Cross two stiles and turn right on to the Purbeck Way. Follow the track up the valley, bending left at Coombe Bottom and right through a gate and up a hill. Go through the gate at the top, then bear right on to a track. At the farm turn left then right to meet the road. Cross and turn left down the track, 'Purbeck Way'. Stay on this to the bottom of the hill passing through a kissing gate part way down. By fir trees turn left, cross a footbridge and turn right. Pass a farm as you go through three more gates and head on to the heath.

3 After a footbridge, go straight on over Corfe Common towards the castle. Bear left at a marker, and right to a gate. Cross the B3069, go through a gate and straight on, later bearing right behind houses. Go through a gate and follow the path towards the village centre. After it narrows turn right, through a gate, and go across fields into a playground. Turn left then right into West Street to the square.

4 Turn left by the castle on the path below the walls. Go left up the road and soon left again by a gate and over a stile. Cross the fields to a car park. Here bear right, then right again on to West Street. At the end, go straight on over a cattle grid. Bear left on a path across the heath. Cross duckboards and go uphill, bearing right, as you near the top, between a stone block and a tumulus. Go straight down the other side and through a gate. Cross two bridges and go up the path between trees and over a stile. Go ahead across a field, over another stile and into a green droving lane. Cross next field, go straight over a road and up the hill. Walk up the next field, heading towards Kingston church tower.

5 At the top, enter a gate and turn right. Immediately after a junction of lanes, turn left, up through some trees, then bear left to a road. Turn right, soon taking the track on the left, signposted 'Houns Tout'. Follow this to the sea and along the exposed cliff tops. Descend steps, then cross a stile at the bottom. Head inland to a road. Turn right and follow it round, bearing left on to a track 'Coastal Path'. Beside a house bear right, downhill. Go through a gate and continue ahead up the road. Where this swings right, bear left to Beacon Bottom. After 0.25 mile (400m) turn right over the stile and retrace your steps to the car park.

Route facts

DISTANCE/TIME 9 miles (14.5 km) 3h45

MAP OS Explorer OL15 Purbeck & South Dorset

START Worth Matravers car park (just north of village; honesty box), grid ref: SY 974776

TRACKS Village lanes, rocky lanes (slippery after rain), moorland tracks, grassy paths, cliff path; 16 stiles

GETTING TO THE START Worth Matravers is 3 miles (4.8km) south of Corfe Castle. Turn off the A351 south of Corfe on to the B3069. Worth Matravers is 1 mile (1.6km) ahead.

THE PUB The Greyhound Inn, The Square, Corfe Castle. Tel: 01929 480205

❶ The main A351 through Corfe is busy and dangerous.

CORFE CASTLE MAP REF SY9682

Corfe Castle is the best-known village on the so-called Isle of Purbeck, and is packed with pubs, tea rooms and little shops that make it a magnet for summer visitors, who are rewarded with excellent walking in the area.

The huge and toothy ruin of Corfe Castle seems to fill the gap in the wall of the Purbeck Hills with its presence. It has a grim history. In AD 978 a youthful King Edward (the Martyr) was murdered here by his stepmother; his body was buried without ceremony at Wareham, while his half-brother took the throne as Ethelred II (the Unready). However, stories of miracles soon resulted in the exhumation of Edward's body. It was transported to Shaftesbury, where an abbey grew up in his honour.

Around 1106 the big square Norman keep was built, to defend against raiders from the sea and to impress the local populace. King John used it as a lifelong prison for his niece Eleanor, a potential threat to his throne. Edward II, deposed by his wife, was imprisoned here briefly.

During the Civil War the castle's owner, Sir John Bankes, eventually sided with the King, leaving his spirited wife, Mary, with a handful of women and just five men, to fight off a siege in 1642. History books state that the 500-strong Parliamentarian army stripped all the lead from the church roof to make their bullets, and stored their gunpowder and shot in the organ pipes, but they failed to take the castle. After a second siege, the castle was betrayed in 1646 by one of its defenders, and after it was abandoned it was destroyed to prevent its use again.

South of Corfe, Worth Matravers is a picturesque village of lichen-encrusted grey cottages, complete with duck pond. Men from here have worked in the local quarries for centuries, and Purbeck marble (in fact a type of limestone) from this area was famously sent inland for the building of Salisbury Cathedral. The Square & Compass, an old fashioned pub with smoked beams and a big stone hearth, is a favourite with walkers. On the nearby cliffs stands 800-year-old St Adhelm's Chapel, a sturdy, buttressed brown cube, that has only one tiny little window. Near the coastguard station is a steel memorial to the brilliant work of radar developers here in 1940–42.

CRANBORNE CHASE
MAP REF ST9317

Cranborne Chase covers an area of around 100sq miles (260sq km) of the long chalk massif that straddles the Dorset–Wiltshire border to the east of Shaftesbury. It was once a popular royal hunting preserve, but is now mostly rolling grassland with pockets of mixed woodland. On the northwestern flanks, Fontmell and Melbury downs are particularly beautiful, and covered with butterflies in summer. To the southeast lie a string of attractive little villages, including Tarrants Gunville and Hinton, and Chettle. Sixpenny Handley has one of the oddest names in England – which alone justifies a visit – but if you go there expecting a romantic 1950s throwback, be prepared for a surprise. Much of the old village was destroyed by fire in 1892; today it is a bold, lively modern village with lots of new housing.

■ Visit

SMEDMORE HOUSE

The Clavell family have been at Smedmore since the 13th century, and Smedmore House, a handsome twin-bayed affair dating from 1761, keeps a firm eye on activities in the bay still. It is occasionally open in high summer when its attractive gardens are in bloom. The Clavell Tower folly, now dangerously close to the crumbling cliff edge, is currently the subject of a major rescue project.

Compared with other parts of Dorset, there are few settlements here, a sign of the feudal state in which the land was held until 1830. After the last Ice Age, Dorset was smothered in a growth of broadleaved woodland, including species such as oak, ash and elm, known as 'native'. As the human population grew and spread, this woodland was gradually cleared for its timber and to make way for agricultural land. The hunting 'forest' of Cranborne Chase claimed by William the Conqueror therefore included open sections of heath, downland, scrub and rough pasture, as well as patches of remaining woodland.

Little of the original forest remains on the Chase – most woods show signs of mixed planting and many generations of coppicing, which was designed to produce a continuous supply of timber for everyday use. The effects of planting for timber in the later 18th century can be seen in the widespread stands of non-native beech across the Chase. Trees for timber were planted compactly to encourage tall, straight growth with a minimum of interruption from side branches. The pursuit of fallow deer on the Chase provided the mainstay of royal sport, and they can still be seen here, most visible in the early evening.

In the early 18th century, the hunting rights on Cranborne Chase passed to the powerful Pitt-Rivers family, who proceeded to rule the area like a feudal manor. Operating under the so-called Chase Law it became a byway for many smugglers and a refuge for criminals. In 1830, after much local campaigning, Chase Law was abandoned.

KIMMERIDGE BAY

MAP REF SY9189

There's a bleakness about Kimmeridge Bay that the energy of the youthful windsurfers riding the waves and the cheerful picture of families pottering in the rock pools can't quite dispel. Giant slabs of black rock shelving out to sea, with crumbling cliffs topped by clumps of wild cabbage, create something of this mood, and the slow, steady nodding donkey-head of the oil well above a terrace of unmistakably industrial cottages reinforces it.

Iron Age tribes first spotted the potential of the band of bituminous shale that runs through Kimmeridge, polishing it up into different blackstone ornaments, and even chair and table legs. The shale, permeated with crude oil, is also known as Kimmeridge coal, but many attempts to work it on an industrial scale failed, including alum extraction (for dyeing) in the 16th century, and using the coal to fuel a glassworks in the 17th century. The shale was worked in the 19th century, and for one brief period the street lights of Paris were lit by gas extracted from the shale oil, but nothing lasted for very long. Since 1959 British Petroleum has drilled 1,716 feet (523m) below the sea; its beam engine sucks out some 80 barrels of crude oil a day. Transported to the Wytch Farm collection point, near Corfe, the oil is then pumped to Hamble, ready to be shipped around the world.

Its combination of clear, shallow water, double low tides and accessible rocky ledges makes Kimmeridge an ideal choice for an underwater nature reserve. The double low tide is at its best in the afternoons – the water may stay low all afternoon, allowing optimum access to the fingers of rock that stretch out into the bay, revealing an amazing world of rock pools and gullies alive with seaweeds, anemones and creatures that include crabs, blennies and the more bizarre pipe-fish. Learn more at the Fine Foundation Marine Centre. Kimmeridge is part of the Smedmore estate, and accessed via a private toll road.

In contrast to Kimmeridge, Tyneham, over the hill, is a cosy farming village clustered around its church in a glorious valley. As you get up close, however, you realise that it's impossibly neat, like an idealised film set. Inside the church is an exhibition to explain all: the villagers were asked to give up their homes in December 1943 for the 'war effort', and Tyneham became absorbed into the vast acreage of the Lulworth Ranges, part of the live firing range. It is a touching memorial, though perhaps nothing can make up for the fact that the villagers were never allowed back to their homes.

KINGSTON LACY MAP REF ST9802

Kingston Lacy is an elegant mansion dating from 1663 and is set in extensive parkland northwest of Wimborne. The house, which has a particularly fine collection of paintings, was built for the Bankes family after the destruction of Corfe Castle in the Civil War, and the house was then remodelled in the 19th century by Sir Charles Barry. One of the most unusual chambers is the Spanish Room, with its walls adorned with gilded leather. On the 8,000-acre (3,240ha) estate, Conegar Capers is a woodland play area for younger children, and there are lots of good waymarked walks.

One of the most obvious legacies of the Roman invasion of Britain in AD 43 is the network of straight military roads that they constructed across the country. Four of the most important Roman routes met at the hub of Badbury Rings, just north of Kingston Lacy. The most famous and visible of these is Ackling Dyke, the major road which linked London (Londinium) with Old Sarum (Sorviodunum), Dorchester (Durnovaria, the *civitas* or Roman capital of the Dorset area) and Exeter (Iscarduniorum).

Badbury Rings was a massive hill-fort occupying a spectacular vantage point. Bronze Age burial barrows in the area confirm a settlement in around 2000 BC, and the rings and ditches date from the 6th century BC, when Dorset was inhabited by the Durotriges tribe. It is a peaceful spot, softened by the trees on top, a recent replanting to replicate what was there in 1761. The hill-fort is approached via a magnificent avenue of beeches planted by William Bankes.

LULWORTH COVE

MAP REF SY8380

Lulworth Cove is an almost perfectly circular bay in the rolling line of limestone cliffs that form Dorset's southern coast. It provides a safe anchorage for small fishing boats and pleasure craft, and a sun-trap of safe water for summer bathers. The wave-polished grey, black and red pebbles of the shingle beach, from wren's egg to ostrich egg in size, are reminiscent of childhood jars of pebble sweets. To the west, along the South West Coast Path, lie rolling, chalky downs and the landmark of Durdle Door, below the cliffs. To the east lie Worbarrow and Mupe bays.

The geology of the area is intriguing, and a visit to the Heritage Centre in the village will help you to identify the various rock formations. The oldest layer is the gleaming white Portland stone, much employed by Christopher Wren in his rebuilding of London. It is a fine-grained oolite around 140 million years old, consisting of tightly compressed fossilised shells, and occasionally throws up giant flat-coiled ammonites, called titanite, which may be seen incorporated decoratively into many house walls across Purbeck. Above this is a thick layer of Purbeck marble, a rich limestone where dinosaur, reptile and fish fossils are usually found. The soft layer above this consists of Wealden beds – a belt of colourful sedimentary clays, silts and sands that are unstable and prone to landslips when exposed. Crumbly white chalk overlays this, the remains of microscopic sea creatures and shells deposited over a long period of time when a deep sea covered much of Dorset, some 75 million years ago.

The Fossil Forest in the sea cliffs east of Lulworth Cove is an intriguing oddity, but don't go looking for stone trees. What you see are the stone rings where sediment has bubbled up around tree-trunks that rotted away millions of years ago. Together with the fossilised soil discovered beneath the tree boles, they give an insight into Jurassic life here, 135 million years ago.

Lulworth Castle Park at nearby East Lulworth was a hunting lodge, built four-square in 1608 with pepperpot towers. Gutted by fire in 1929, it is now a handsome shell, and still only partly restored. Other attractions on the estate include a circular chapel, an animal farm and an adventure playground for children, and summer jousting events.

Nearly 200 rescued and endangered apes and monkeys have found a new, welcoming home at Monkey World, a few miles north of Wool. The park has 65 acres (26ha) of woodland, where the monkeys can recuperate in a safe environment made specifically for them.

■ Insight

THE DOLLS HOUSE

As you make your way down to the pretty harbour in Lulworth, look out for the tiny baby-blue timber Dolls House. It is a restored Victorian fisherman's cottage dating from 1861, now a fishing museum, and you may find it difficult to believe that 11 children were raised in this tiny house. Contrast its cramped simplicity with the cottage orné opposite, with big diamond-pane windows and a cosy thatched roof.

MILTON ABBAS MAP REF ST8102

It is the natural order of villages to grow over generations, to spread out a little, to develop secret corners, and to reflect different ages, abilities and tastes in its buildings. Rarely do you find a village quite so symmetrical as Milton Abbas, whose regular whitewashed houses, identical in design, are placed neatly on either side of a narrow defile, thatched cowl opposite thatched cowl. It's an unnatural and slightly eerie sight. On closer inspection, you see that rebels have managed to sneak on a porch here, a coat of cream-coloured paint there, but nothing to seriously spoil the effect of planned perfection. There appear to have been no concessions either on houses that were once a bakery and a forge, although the tailor's house had bow windows for extra light.

The answer lies with the great house round the corner, the dream of Joseph and Caroline Damer, who bought Milton Abbey in 1752. It was on a fabulous site, but the house left much to be desired. In 1771 they decided to build something grander, to include a landscaped park by 'Capability' Brown. But the ugly and untidy township around the abbey was spoiling the view, and would have to go.

And so a new hamlet of thatched cottages was built out of sight in a narrow valley, and the villagers were moved, whether they liked it or not. The houses look generous, but in fact each little block was two independent family dwellings, separated by a shared central hall. What the villagers had to say about the near-vertical valley walls behind their shiny new homes is not recorded,

but some steep terraced gardens were eventually dug out, and are one of the attractive features of Milton Abbas today.

The Damers are buried in splendour in the abbey church; their house, never the architectural success they had hoped for, became a school in 1954.

Nearby Winterborne Clenston is altogether more organic, combining a pretty Victorian rectory with a magnificent Tudor manor house and a medieval tithe barn with a steep chequerboard roof of alternating red and black squares. The Gothic church of St Nicholas, dating from 1840, is a perfectly proportioned miniature.

POOLE MAP REF SZ0291

Unlike its frivolous and glitzy neighbour, Bournemouth, Poole has an ancient and serious heart that gives it a different character. It grew up in the Middle Ages as the main port on one of the world's greatest and safest natural harbours, taking over in maritime importance from Wareham. Today it is still very much a working port, with marinas packed out with expensive sailing yachts, a small surviving fishing fleet, many productive boatyards creating some of the costliest and sleekest luxury motorboats made in the world, and cross-Channel ferries – the biggest craft to negotiate the narrow entrance to the harbour at Sandbanks.

The best place to start an exploration of Old Poole is the Quay – the attractive old waterfront, with views across the harbour and more immediately, to the boatyards. The Cockle Trail is a walking trail around the historic town – pick up a leaflet at the tourist office.

At the western end the Quay is lined with stylish old buildings, including the brick Customs House of 1813, as well as the pillared Coastguard office of 1820, all on an appealingly small scale. There are old pubs along here, too, including the Poole Arms with its green-glazed tile frontage, and the handsome King's Head, set slightly back at the lower end of the High Street. This is Poole's main shopping street, lined with small and largely practical shops – for bigger high-street names head inland to the modern Dolphin Shopping Centre. As you stroll eastwards along the Quay, past the town marina with its gleaming moored yachts, you soon reach the rustier hulks of the fishing fleet. There is a small museum in a wooden shed to explore, its paint faded and peeling – it is the home of the old Thomas Kirk Wright lifeboat, which took part as one of the flotilla of 'Little Ships' in the brave evacuation of Allied soldiers from Dunkirk in May, 1940.

Between the Quay and the end tip of the sheltering sandspit of Sandbanks, the coastline seems like one long haven or park dedicated to varied watersports and sailing. Paragliding, wakeboarding and kitesurfing are favourite activities in these shallow, sheltered waters.

The peninsula of Sandbanks is favoured by millionaires. Property here is so desirable that house prices match those of Manhattan and central Tokyo.

Laid inland from Sandbanks amid elegant and spacious Edwardian villas, Compton Acres is a huge, privately owned pleasure garden established in the 1920s. As well as themed gardens, which include a Wooded Valley, a pretty Grotto, a Water Garden and Roman and Japanese gardens, the 10-acre (4ha) site also has two restaurants for fine dining, a delicatessen and craft and gift shops.

STUDLAND MAP REF SZ0383

The glorious sands in Studland Bay are justly famous, and attract over a million visitors a year, so it's worth getting up early to have them to yourself. You are unlikely to be alone for long, though. As you progress up the beach, getting warmer, you can shed your clothes with impunity, for the upper stretch opens its arms to naturists – and even on a bright winter's morning you'll spot brave souls sunbathing naked in the shelter of the marram-covered dunes. Offshore, big, sleek motor boats let rip as they emerge from the constraints of Poole Harbour. Watch out, too, for the orange and blue of the Poole lifeboat on manoeuvres, and the yellow and black pilot boat nipping out to lead in the tankers. Jet-skiers zip around the more sedate sailing yachts, all dodging the small fishing boats. It's a perfect seaside harmony, complete with wheedling, soaring gulls.

Behind the beach lies the old rugged heath, part of the same nature reserve that is in the care of English Nature and the National Trust. They are currently working together on a programme of restoration, reclaiming heath that had become farmland, and clearing scrub and maintaining controlled grazing to prevent it all reverting to woodland. All six of Britain's reptiles – common lizard, sand lizard, smooth snake, adder, grass snake, slow worm – live on the heath.

Durdle Door and Lulworth Cove

An exhilarating walk on a stunning stretch of coastline visiting Durdle Door, a spectacular natural rock arch in the sea, and Lulworth Cove before turning inland and skirting the village of West Lulworth. The white chalk that breaks through the soil here underlies Dorset's famous downland and is seen in the exposed soft, eroded cliffs at White Nothe.

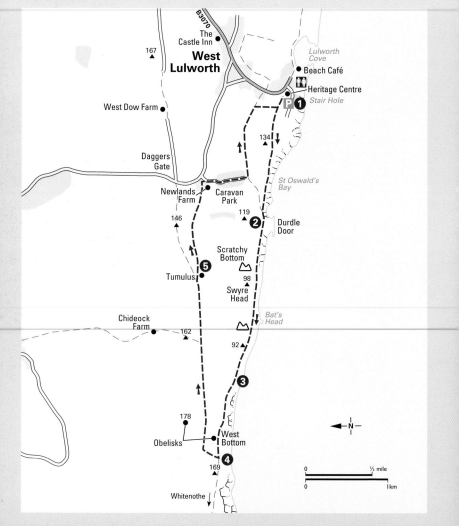

Route Directions

1 Find the gate at the back of the car park. Pass through this to take the broad, paved footpath that leads up some shallow steps to the top of the first hill. Continue along the brow, and down the other side. Pass below a caravan park and through a gate.

2 Reach the cove of Durdle Door, almost enclosed from the sea by a line of rocks. A flight of steps leads down to the sea here, but carry on walking straight ahead on the coast path and the natural stone arch of the Door itself is revealed in a second cove below you. The mass of Swyre Head looms close and yes, that is the path you're going to take, ascending straight up the side. Walk down to the bottom then climb back up to Swyre Head. The path leads steeply down again on the other side, to a short stretch overlooking Bat's Head. Climb the next steep hill. Continue along the path behind the cliffs, where the land tilts away from the sea.

3 The path climbs more gently up the next hill. Pass a navigation obelisk on the right, and follow the path as it curves round the contour above West Bottom.

4 At a marker stone that indicates Whitenothe ahead turn right, through a gate, and follow a fence inland. The path curves round so you're walking parallel with the coast on level greensward. Pass three stone embrasures with shell sculptures inside, and a second obelisk. Go through a gate. Now keep straight ahead along the top of the field and across a crossing of paths, signed to Daggers Gate. Go through a gateway and straight on. The path starts to descend gently. In the next field the path becomes more of a track. Bear right to pass close by a tumulus and reach a gate.

5 Cross this and walk along the top of the field, above Scratchy Bottom. Cross a stile into a green lane leading to Newlands Farm. Follow it round to the right, and turn right into the caravan park. Go straight ahead on the road through here. At the far side go through a gate and turn left, signed to West Lulworth. Stay along the field-edge and walk above a farm lane, around the end of the hill. Keep straight on at the fingerpost and reach the gate above the car park. Turn left and retrace your route.

Route facts

DISTANCE/TIME 6.75 miles (10.9km) 3h

MAP OS Explorer OL15 Purbeck & South Dorset

START Pay-and-display car park (busy), Lulworth Cove grid ref: SY 821800

TRACKS Stone path, grassy tracks, tarmac, stiles

GETTING TO THE START
From the A352 west of Wareham take the B3070 south for East Lulworth and continue to West Lulworth. Continue to Lulworth Cove and the car park there.

THE PUB The Castle Inn, West Lulworth.
Tel: 01929 400311;
www.thecastleinn-lulworth cove.co.uk

❶ Take heed of warning signs – steep paths (up and down) and cliff edges. A short walk but really for fitter, older children.

Poole & the Isle of Purbeck

The Isle of Purbeck is the fascinating area to the west of Poole, a landlocked island of high hills and sea cliffs. The route entails a complete circuit of Poole Harbour, with a short ferry ride at the end. On the way you will see lovely villages and a deserted village, sheltered bays, a ruined castle, seaside resorts, a seaside pier and the long sandy beach of Studland.

Route Directions

Explore the quayside at Poole, with its shops, pubs and the Poole pottery factory outlet.

1 Leave Poole town centre and follow the signs for Hamworthy and Poole Bridge. Cross the bridge, by the Sunseeker boatyard, and continue towards Hamworthy and Rockley Park. After 2.5 miles (4km) pass under two railway bridges, with Upton Park signed to your left. Continue through Upton, and at the double roundabout by the clock tower turn left, signed 'Lytchett Minster'. Pass through Lytchett Minster. At the roundabout with the A35, go straight ahead, signed 'A351 Wareham'. Continue ahead across several roundabouts and through traffic lights, following signs to Wareham. Go straight on at the next roundabout, signed 'Corfe Castle', and bear left at the next roundabout, and follow signs for Wareham. Stop in Wareham to explore this historic town.

2 In Wareham continue down the high street, then cross the river. Continue to Stoborough and bear right, signed 'Creech'. At the junction with the A351 turn left and immediately right, signed 'Creech, Steeple and Kimmeridge'. Turn right onto a minor road, signed to East and West Lulworth.
The route passes through an area of farmland and open heath that is typical of the area, with pine forests, and parkland at East Holme. There is a stunning view of the long chalk ridge of the Purbeck Hills off to your left.

3 After 2.5 miles (4km), turn left for East Lulworth – look out for tanks crossing on this part of the army training area. Continue through the village of East Lulworth. At the T-junction turn left and go on through West Lulworth village to Lulworth Cove.
Park on the right, by the heritage centre, to explore the cove and coastal path.

4 Retrace your route for 3 miles (4.8km) back up the hill and almost to the gates of Lulworth Castle. Turn right here, and take the next narrow turning right, signed 'Tyneham Village'.
This winding road rises along the back of the ridge and up to the crest, with superb views across the country inland.

5 After 4.5 miles (7.2km), Whiteways Viewpoint is on your right.
Enjoy views down over the coast and Kimmeridge Bay, and to Poole Harbour straight ahead of you.

6 Continue, and a turning circle on the left marks the tight right turn down to Tyneham village. Follow the road down to the church. Explore the deserted village which was evacuated in 1943.

7 Return up the road to the turning circle and turn right. Just before another viewpoint turn right towards Steeple and Kimmeridge. The narrow road descends sharply. Turn right, signed to Kimmeridge and the sea. The road crosses a valley and goes up a ridge before descending to pass by Smedmore House. Finally, it zig-zags down through Kimmeridge village. Note: a toll is payable if you want to continue down to the beach car park on Kimmeridge Bay. The pebble beach here, with its long rock ledges and numerous rock pools, is popular with families and water sports enthusiasts.

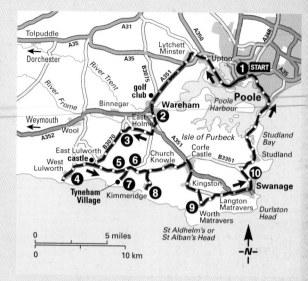

8 Retrace your route back across the valley and turn right, signed to Church Knowle and Corfe Castle. After 1.5 miles (2.4km) pass through Church Knowle. Continue towards Corfe, circling the base of the castle mound, and turn right to Swanage on the A351. Make your way through the centre of Corfe village. On the other side of the village turn right, signed to Langton Matravers. Cross the Common. Follow the road left, and soon turn right, which is signed 'Worth Matraver's. Continue for a mile (1.6km), passing the quarry on your right. Park your car in the car park just above Worth Matravers. Walk down the hill and

bear right to visit the duck pond and the Church of St Nicholas.

9 Turn left at the Square and Compass pub, at the sign to Langton Matravers. Turn right at the main road and descend to Langton Matravers. At the junction with the A351 turn right and then follow signs for Swanage town centre and to the beach.
The traditional seaside resort of Swanage has a gently shelving sandy beach and a Victorian pier.

10 Leave Swanage on the coast road, signed 'Studland, Poole and Bournemouth via toll ferry'. After 3 miles

(4.8km) turn right for Studland on the B3351. Continue to the ferry crossing Studland Heath.
The toll ferry crossing to Sandbanks takes about 10 minutes only, but expect to queue in high season. Follow the B3369 coast road, past Compton Acres, back into the centre of Poole.

PUNCH & JUDY
SWANAGE
SHOWS DAILY
12.30 2.30 4.00
Adults & Children
£1.00

SWANAGE MAP REF SZ0378

In the early 19th century Swanage was a small, bustling industrial port shipping stone from the 60 or more quarries in the area. A growing fashion for sea-bathing would in time change the focus of the town for ever. The real changes to the face of Swanage came, however, with the extraordinary collecting habit of one George Burt, a contractor with an eye for ornate architecture.

With his uncle John Mowlem, a local stonemason and philanthropist, Burt shipped marble from the old quarries of Purbeck up to London, where many old buildings were being knocked down to make way for new construction. He was reluctant to see such fine stonework discarded, so Burt salvaged large whole pieces, transported them back to Dorset as ballast, and re-erected them in his home town, giving Swanage an 'instant' architectural heritage.

The Town Hall is a prime example of Burt's influence. He had donated a reasonably plain and simple building to the town in 1872; but in 1883 he added a façade by Wren, which he had rescued from the Mercers' Hall in London's Cheapside. In a park near the pier you can see a grand archway removed from Hyde Park Corner, and three statues and some columns rescued from Billingsgate Market. There is also an absurd but rather elegant clock tower, removed from the south end of London Bridge in 1867, where it had been set as a memorial to the Duke of Wellington.

Durleston Castle is an original folly by Burt dating from 1887, designed from the start as a clifftop restaurant on Durleston Head. Facts and figures from around the world are carved into great stone slabs set into the walls below. Burt added a large, segmented stone globe of the world. It is grey and rather disappointing, but nevertheless in a beautiful spot where you can sit during the evening, watching the sunset fade the sea into the sky, with the lighthouse at the end of the Needles winking from across the water.

At Studland Museum and Heritage Centre you can learn more about the area, including tales of smuggling and the development of Purbeck's stone quarrying industry. And for a nominal fee, try the delights of Swanage's Victorian pier, which announces penny-in-the-slot machines and 'Wot the butler saw' – no seaside visit can be complete without it. The pier suffered in the past from neglect and threat of demolition, but is now undergoing restoration.

TOLPUDDLE MAP REF SY7995

Tolpuddle is a peaceful village tucked in the fold of a hill beside the A35. It is associated with a political revolt in the 19th century, celebrated with the Martyrs' Museum, commemorated in the name of the local pub, and marked at various other points.

The Martyrs' Tree stands on the little green at the heart of Tolpuddle. It was a meeting point for the Friendly Society of Agricultural Labourers, a group formed to peaceably lobby their masters for much better pay, at a time when a local labourer's wage was just seven shillings a week – around three shillings below what was paid elsewhere in Dorset, and barely enough to feed a family on. Such unions were unlawful, and George and James Loveless, Thomas and John Standfield, James Brine and James Hammett were picked out as ringleaders and troublemakers, and convicted at Dorchester in 1834.

The six men were duly exiled, but their case was unusual. Despite their conviction for 'administering unlawful oaths', their seven-year sentences were quashed after public outrage, and the Tolpuddle Martyrs were pardoned. The processes of law and communication were slow in those times, and it was five years before they all returned home.

George Loveless, a well-spoken Methodist lay preacher whose statue sits outside the museum, had developed a taste for life beyond these valleys, and after his return he emigrated to Canada with four of the others. James Hammet was the only one to die in the village, and his grave is in the local churchyard.

Between 1800 and 1850 some 1,800 individuals convicted of political crimes were shipped out to Australia, effectively silencing dangerous elements.

Athelhampton, one of England's most majestic old mansions, is just down the road to the west, and well worth a visit. Parts of it date from 1485, and the house is stuffed with treasures, from Tudor architecture in the Great Hall to a carved Charles I tester bed. Allow time to explore the world-famous gardens with their yew topiary and fountains.

WAREHAM MAP REF SY9387

Wareham bills itself as a Saxon walled town, but a great fire in 1762 destroyed many of the older buildings, and what you see today in the centre is mainly Georgian. The town has had a chequered history, its status as the major trading port on Poole Harbour making it quite vulnerable to attacks from marauding Vikings, and then undermined when the River Frome silted up badly during the Middle Ages.

One survivor from the town's earliest heyday is St Martin's Church. Dating from around 1030, it's the oldest church in Dorset, and stands on the northern section of the ancient town walls. It has some remarkable fragments of 12th-century frescoes, and now houses an effigy of T E Lawrence, by sculptor Eric Kennington, in Arab costume and with his head resting on a camel saddle. Learn more about Lawrence of Arabia in the redbrick Town Museum on the High Street. This broad and gracious street is the main thoroughfare of the town, leading down to the river, and is lined with interesting shops and eating places.

Stroll along the quiet heath road through Ridge, once a busy river port in its own right, to the hamlet of Arne, 3 miles (4.8km) away near the shores of Poole Harbour. Many of the houses here

Splashdown Water Park
Tower Park, northeast of
Poole on A3049.
Tel: 01202 716000;
www.splashdownpoole.co.uk

■ SHOPPING

Poole Markets
Street market, High Street,
and Farmer's Market,
Falkland Square, every Thu.

**Swanage Market &
Farmers' Market**
Main beach car park, Tue,
Easter–Autumn.

Wareham Market
Every Thu.

**Wimborne Market &
Farmers' Market**
Friday; also flea market
Sat–Sun.

■ PERFORMING ARTS

Pavilion Theatre
Westover Road,
Bournemouth.
Tel: 01202 456400

**Bournemouth International
Centre**
Exeter Road.
Tel: 01202 456400

Pier Theatre
Pier, Bournemouth.
Tel: 08445 763000

■ SPORTS & ACTIVITIES

Adrenalin Days
Tel: 07881 586575.
A variety of powerboat and
charter boat trips that leave
from Poole Harbour.

Shoc
Bourn
Tel: 01
www.d
Speedb
Snowtr
Matcha
Tel: 012
www.sn
CRUISES
Blue Line
Sailings fr
Tel: 01202
www.bluel
Brownsea
Tel: 01929 4
brownseaisl
The Dorset
Bournemout
Tel: 08454 68
www.dorsetc
Ferry services
CYCLE HIRE
First Floor, Do
Shopping Cent
Tel: 01202 6801
www.cycle-path
FISHING
Poole Sea Angli
Rear of 5 High St
Tel: 01202 676597
pooleseaanglingo
WATERSPORTS
FC Watersports A
by Sandbanks Hote
Sandbanks, Poole.
Tel: 01202 708283;
www.fcwatersports.
Rockley Watersport
Rockley Point Sailing
west of Poole.

---

were demolished during World War II
when the army used the village as a
training ground, and what's left remains
in sleepy retirement. There is a 13th-
century church to explore, and a nature
reserve where rare Dartford warblers
breed and nightjars sing.

North of Wareham, at Sandford, is
Farmer Palmer's, a great family farm
park, complete with hands-on animal
feeding, milking cows, tractor rides and
amusements – perfect for the under-8s.

WIMBORNE MINSTER

MAP REF **SU0200**

This attractive old market town on the
River Stour made its fortunes in ancient
times on the profits of wool. Its most
distinctive feature is the Minster Church
of St Cuthberga, whose squat, square
towers dominate the town centre. Its
foundation dates back to AD 705, though
the present building dates from some
400 years later. One of the town's most
fascinating elements is the library, which
was founded in 1686 for the free use of
the townspeople, and consists of 350
(mainly theological) volumes. To prevent
the theft of these items, the books were
chained to the shelves – workhouse
orphans made the chains. The Quarter
Jack clock on the west tower is a
much-loved local icon, with its brightly
painted soldier striking the quarter
hours with a hammer.

The nearby village Cornmarket, is a
sheltered square, with an old pub, the
White Hart, that becomes the centre of
activities around the Folk Festival. The
King's Head Hotel on the old main
Square was formerly a coaching inn.

■ Insight

THE RIVER STOUR

The Stour supports a rich variety of
wildlife. Most obvious are the birds, with
mallards and mute swans on the water,
moorhens, warblers and buntings in the
tall reed beds, and grey herons and exotic
white egrets fishing in the shallows. Trout,
roach, perch, dace, minnows and eels live
in the water, and in summer look out for
orange tip, peacock and clouded yellow
butterflies, dragonflies and damselflies.

The Priest's House Museum on the
High Street is a medieval house with
some later additions, originally built for
use by the priests at the Minster but
was later occupied by a succession of
different tradespeople, including an
ironmonger, a tobacconist and a printer.
It is full of the domestic paraphernalia
of years gone by, including a Victorian
kitchen and a tinsmith's workshop. The
walled garden, which leads gently down
to the river, is a particular delight.

Wimborne has its own model town,
carefully created to 1:10 scale some 50
years ago, which is the primary focus for
children's activities such as a putting
lawn, and special events for all ages
throughout the year.

East of Wimborne, at Hampreston,
lie Knoll Gardens, a superb modern
garden and specialist nursery displaying
grasses, perennials and much more. To
the northeast lies Stapehill, the site of
a 19th-century abbey now transformed
into extensive, beautiful formal as well
as informal gardens, with a countryside
museum and farmyard. There are also
resident craftspeople.

■ TOURIST INFORMATION CENTRES

Bournemouth
Westover Road.
Tel: 0845 051 1700;
www.bournemouth.co.uk

Poole
Enefco House, Poole Quay.
Tel: 01202 253253;
www.pooletourism.com

Swanage
The White House,
Shore Road.
Tel: 01929 422885;
www.swanage.gov.uk

Wareham
Holy Trinity Church,
South Street.
Tel: 01929 552740;
www.purbeck.gov.uk

Wimborne
29 High Street.
Tel: 01202 886116;
www.ruraldorset.com

■ PLACES OF INTEREST

Arne RSPB Reserve
Wareham.
Tel: 01929 553360

**Athelhampton House
& Gardens**
Tel: 01305 848363;
www.athelhampton.co.uk

**Bournemouth
Aviation Museum**
Bournemouth Airport.
Tel: 01202 473141;
www.aviation-museum.co.uk

Bovington Tank Museum
Tel: 01929 405096;
www.tankmuseum.org

Brownse
Offshore
Tel: 01202

Clouds Hil
Near Bovin
Tel: 01929

Compton Ac
Tel: 01202 7
www.compt

Corfe Castle
Tel: 01929 48

Corfe Model
Tel: 01929 48
www.corfecas
co.uk

Fine Foundatic
Marine Centre
Purbeck Marin
Reserve, Kimme
Tel: 01929 48104

Kingston Lacy (
Wimborne Minst
Tel: 01202 88340

Knoll Gardens
Hampreston, near
Tel: 01202 873931
www.knollgardens

Lulworth Castle &
East Lulworth, War
Tel: 0845 450 1054;
www.lulworth.com

Monkey World
Wool, near Wareham
Tel: 0800 456600;
www.monkeyworld.or

Oceanarium
Pier Approach,
West Beach,
Bournemouth.
Tel: 01202 311993;
www.oceanarium.co.uk

e-modeltown.
com

Tea Rooms

All Fired Up Café
The Square,
35–37 Bourne Avenue,
Bournemouth BH2 6DT
Tel: 01202 558030;
www.allfiredupceramics.co.uk
This is a café with a huge
difference – tuck into herbal,
fruit or iced teas, Italian
coffee and tasty home-baked
cakes, while you decorate
your own pottery blank. Your
piece will be fired and glazed
to collect a few days later.

Blue Pool and Tea House
Furzebrook, near
Wareham BH20 5AT
Tel: 01929 551408; www.
bluepooltearooms.co.uk
The Blue Pool is a beauty
spot created from an old clay
works, surrounded by 25
acres (10ha) of woodland and
heath. The genteel Tea House
was first opened here in 1935
and boasts its own little
museum. Today it serves
cream teas and light lunches,
and is the perfect stopping
place for refreshments as you
explore the area.

Cavell's Farm Shop
& Café
Kimmeridge, near
Wareham BH20 5PE
Tel: 01929 480701
Enjoy a Dorset cream tea in
pleasant surroundings. All
of the teas are Fairtrade and
organic, and there's a great
shop selling produce from
the farm.

The Courtyard Tea Room
Model Village, The Square,
Corfe Castle BH20 5EZ
Tel: 01929 481234
Home-cooked food is the
order of the day at this tea
room in the middle of Corfe
village. As well as cream teas
and delicious cakes, you can
tuck into daily lunchtime
specials. In fine weather,
you can eat out under the
shady umbrellas in the
17th-century courtyard.

Pubs

The Bankes Arms Hotel
Watery Lane,
Studland BH19 3AU
Tel: 01929 450225
Once the haunt of smugglers,
this creeper-clad inn is
renowned for its large menu
of fresh fish and seafood,
including fresh mussels,
crab gratin and lobster
dishes. There are meat
options, too, such as lamb
noisettes in mint, honey
and orange sauce. Each
year the pub hosts a beer
festival, with around 60
real ales on tap accompanied
by music, Morris dancing
and stone carving in the
pub garden.

The Castle Inn
Main Road,
West Lulworth BH20 5RN
Tel: 01929 400311;
www.lulworthinn.com
Thatched and beamed, this
atmospheric old pub close to
Lulworth Cove is perfectly
placed for walkers and other
visitors. There's an extensive
tiered garden, which fills up
quickly on summer days, and
is especially popular with
families. Dogs are permitted
too. The menu includes some
staples such as chicken, ham
and mushroom pie, seafood
stew, fillet steak with oysters
and a more adventurous beef
bourguignon. Beers include
Ringwood Best.

Langton Arms
Tarrant Monkton DT11 8RX
Tel: 01258 830225;
www.thelangtonarms.co.uk
This lovely old thatched pub
in the centre of the village
has a great reputation for its
food, and is popular with
families year round. The
menu changes frequently,
but includes tasty treats such
as game pie, delicious baked
aubergine with ratatouille and
mozzarella, and locally made
Purbeck ice cream or maybe
profiteroles with butterscotch
sauce. There's a good-sized
beer garden, and a children's
play area.

QUEENS BOWER

New Forest

The New Forest, an ancient Royal hunting forest, was created 'new' by William the Conqueror in 1079 as a preserve for hunting deer. The forest is not all dense woodland, as first-time visitors often expect, but consists largely of heathland, with a rich variety of plant life and animals, including the semi-wild ponies, cattle, donkeys and squirrels. Explore beyond the major tourist spots on foot, by bike or on horseback to discover the magic of the place. There are towns, villages and gardens to visit, and attractions include Beaulieu's famous motor museum and the Solent coast.

3 Walk start point

1 Cycle start point

LEPE

CALSHOT

Unmissable attractions

Witness the 'wild' New Forest ponies roaming through woodland and grazing freely on the rough grass with their foals...learn to sail at one of Lymington's busy sailing schools...admire the gardens at Exbury House, famous for its bold rhododendron blooms...power along tracks on a mountain bike or take a leisurely horse-drawn wagon ride at Burley...throw a line in and catch a crab on Mudeford's pretty little quay...stand by the Rufus Stone, the spot where King William II is supposed to have died...bottle-feed a calf or a kid at Longdown Activity Farm...sit quietly in St Nicholas' church at Brockenhurst, the oldest church in the forest...watch fine thoroughbred racehorses galloping across open ground near Roman Rockbourne.

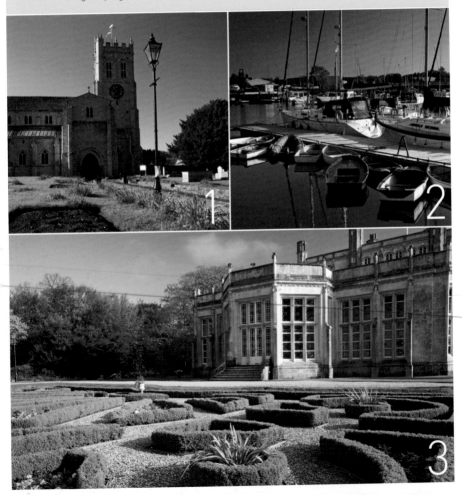

1 Christchurch
The Priory Church has been at the heart of this town for more than 1,200 years, although the present building was begun in the 11th century.

2 Lymington
A leading sailing resort, Lymington has two marinas and is the main port for ferries going to Yarmouth on the Isle of Wight. This lively town with its Georgian and Victorian houses has a great, buzzing atmosphere.

3 Highcliffe Castle
Handsome Grade I listed Highcliffe Castle was acquired by Christchurch Council in 1977 and has undergone much restoration. The grounds were laid out by the landscaper 'Capability' Brown. After your visit you can take the steep steps to the beach below.

4 Cycling in the New Forest
The New Forest Cycle Network links several sites and villages. Most tracks are shared with horse-riders and walkers.

5 Hurst Castle
The castle is one of several defensive southern coast castles erected by Henry VIII. Its low walls were difficult to target from a vessel at sea, and the sturdy structure was able to support heavy artillery.

6 Furzey Gardens
Established in 1922, the lovely gardens incorporate a lake, heathers, and trees and shrubs that give a year-round blaze of colour. The restored Cole Cottage in the grounds dates from the 16th century.

ASHURST MAP REF SU3311

A string of villages lines the A35 between Totton and Lyndhurst. Ashurst, where the housing suddenly stops and the countryside proper begins, was known simply as Lyndhurst Road, like its railway station, until the 1920s, and has developed as prime commuter housing for nearby Southampton. The railway bridge in Ashurst once defined the outer boundary of the New Forest, and this was as close to the hotels and facilities of Lyndhurst that the local landowners would permit the railway to encroach – in fact, the line had to take such a circuitous route that it was nicknamed the 'Weymouth Wanderer'. Further on, to the southwest is the popular campsite of Ashurst Woods.

East of Ashurst, Longdown Activity Farm is a hands-on attraction for all ages, including bottle-feeding goat kids, and calves. Close by is the New Forest Wildlife Park – 25 secluded acres (10ha) of ancient woodland where native species are conserved including red squirrels, harvest mice and barn owls. Special events are family-friendly.

BEAULIEU MAP REF SU3802

The pretty little village of Beaulieu has become synonymous with the National Motor Museum, the private passion of the enterprising then Lord Montagu. His forefathers acquired the Beaulieu estate in Tudor times, with its Cistercian abbey founded in 1204.

The abbey was torn down as part of the Dissolution of the Monasteries countrywide, but the fine cloisters survived and now contain a re-created monastic garden; the refectory became the parish church; and the Domus, the lay brothers' apartments, now houses an exhibition about abbey life. The Tudor house created from the 14th-century gatehouse was reconstructed in the 19th century as the present Palace House, and today shows the domestic workings of a Victorian household. During the Second World War the estate became the top-secret training school for those involved in the Special Operations Executive (SOE), where agents prepared for operations behind enemy lines in occupied France and Europe; a story told in the Secret Army Exhibition.

Lord Montagu first opened this lovely Palace House to the public in 1952, and the brilliant motor museum is dedicated to the memory of his father. It was in fact John Montagu who had successfully petitioned Parliament to abolish the 12mph (19kph) speed limit, among other notable achievements. Today there are more than 250 vintage beauties and stars of the car world to admire in this famous collection, ranging from world record breakers as 'Bluebird' and 'Golden Arrow' to TV favourites including

Insight

NEW FOREST PONIES

New Forest ponies may roam freely, but they are not strictly wild – they belong to the commoners. The Victorians 'improved' the hardy ponies that had grazed the forest for centuries, surviving on a diet of gorse, bracken and brambles, by inter-breeding them with Arab stallions – and now they mainly eat grass. Every autumn the ponies are rounded up for branding and marking, and several times a year ponies are sold at Beaulieu Road Station.

Mr Bean's green Mini, and James Bond's Lotus submarine car from the movie *The Spy Who Loved Me*. A trip on the 'Wheels' pod ride transports you through a century of motoring history, and you can explore the site on a replica 1912 bus or the high-level monorail. Look out for the special events that take place throughout the year.

BREAMORE MAP REF SU1517

Breamore (pronounced 'Bremmer') is an unspoiled village in the northeast corner of the New Forest, with many attractive redbrick, thatched cottages grouped peacefully around its village green. It's a scene jealously guarded from change, and even the village stocks still stand, opposite the Bat and Ball pub. The little church, which dates from about 1000, is one of the most interesting Saxon survivals in Hampshire. The 12th-century porch contains part of the Saxon rood screen, a fine piece of carving, though the figures have been damaged.

The redbrick Elizabethan manor house of Breamore, built on the hillside in 1583, was purchased by Queen Anne's physician Sir Edward Hulse in the 18th century, and is still a family home with collections of paintings, furniture, needlework and porcelain. The Great Hall contains its original carved stone fireplace, and there is a Victorian kitchen with gleaming copperware.

The fascinating Countryside Museum occupies the old farmyard, and has full-size replicas of the village shops that would have made the estate self-sufficient, including a wheelwright's, a blacksmith's and a brewery.

■ Insight

FLYING BOATS

Before the advent of the Second World War, the lumbering forms of flying boats were a familiar sight on Southampton Water. They were based at Hythe, a coastal town northeast of Beaulieu, and flew from here to all parts of the British Empire otherwise inaccessible to aircraft. The parent company was Imperial Airways, which was later nationalised as British Overseas Airways Corporation (BOAC).

BROCKENHURST

MAP REF SU3002

Brockenhurst is a big, pleasant village set amid wooded countryside. On the northern outskirts are two of the largest and loveliest of the New Forest 'lawns', Butts Lawn and Balmer Lawn, the latter overlooked by an elegant hotel.

New Forest churches tend to stand aloof from their villages and ancient Brockenhurst's St Nicholas' Church, hidden away to the east, is no exception. It is reputedly the oldest in the forest, and it was the only one recorded in the 1086 Domesday survey. The yew tree that almost smothers the building has a girth of more than 20 feet (6m) and is known to be more than 1,000 years old.

To the northwest of Brockenhurst is the Rhinefield Ornamental Drive. It features a variety of coniferous trees, including very large redwoods. Forest walks on either side of the drive include a special 'Tall Trees Walk'. Further on, Bolderwood Drive passes close to the famous ancient Knightwood Oak, and the deer sanctuary where platforms offer a view of deer roaming the forest.

FOREST PATH, BURLEY

BUCKLER'S HARD

MAP REF SU4000

Two redbrick, terraced rows of Georgian houses face each other across a wide open space that slopes gently down to the Beaulieu River, on the Beaulieu estate. The area is kept free of cars and presents a peaceful rural scene today. Yet Buckler's Hard, originally called Montagu Town, was the shipyard that built many of the men-of-war for Nelson's fleet, including *Agamemnon*, Nelson's favourite ship. The yard was immensely busy, but overreached itself and folded in 1811. During the Second World War, Buckler's Hard revived its shipbuilding tradition, and some parts of a Mulberry Harbour for the D-Day landings were constructed here. The Maritime Museum displays models of ships built here, and reconstructed cottage interiors offer an insight into the life of 18th-century shipyard workers.

Today, pleasure craft ride the tranquil waters of the Beaulieu River and, in summer, cruises set off from the quay. A riverside walk leads to Beaulieu village.

BURLEY MAP REF SU2102

Burley is an excellent centre for walking, horse-riding and mountain biking. It is an attractive village set high above the River Avon amid the bleak and gaunt heathlands of the western New Forest, where ponies and cattle roam freely. Burley Beacon is the high point of the village, reached by the gravel track from Pound Lane, and from its height the view expands westwards over the Avon Valley. Even better is the view from Castle Hill, topped by an Iron Age camp, at nearby Burley Street. Red deer roam in the grounds of grand Burley Manor.

During the 1950s Burley had its own resident witch, called Sybil Leek, who dressed in black robes with a jackdaw perched on her shoulder. Despite her 'white' tendencies, local resentment at her presence caused her to flee to America. Since then the village has specialised in witchcraft shops as well as the usual range of antiques and other souvenirs. A window in the little church commemorates Constance Applebee, who died in 1981 at the ripe old age of 107. Burley is also home to New Forest Cider, a cider farm with a shop and an exhibition to show how it is made.

CALSHOT MAP REF SU4701

The well-preserved remains of one of Henry VIII's coastal gun-stations, built between 1539 and 1540 against the real threat of a French invasion, stands on a gravel spit jutting out into the Solent. It continued to be of military importance, and today contains a reconstructed barrack room complete with replica 1890s furnishings and a display on the history of the fort. During both world wars it was a Royal Naval Air Station, a base for seaplanes and flying boats, and in the 1920s and 30s the Schneider Trophy seaplane races were held here.

The beach has been designated a country park and adjoins Lepe Country Park to the west, forming a long stretch of shoreline backed by pines and cliff-top walks. The area is known for its habitats – shingle beaches, reed beds, marsh and brackish ponds – which attract extensive marine and bird life.

A New Forest loop from Burley

This route takes you through the heart of the bustling New Forest village of Burley, with its antiques shops, tea rooms and horse-drawn wagon rides then joins the Castleman cycle trail where you can experience the surrounding heathland from a level stretch of old railway line. There are good opportunities for birding, and you can visit the Old Station tea rooms at Holmsley.

Route Directions

1 Turn right out of the car park, stop at the next road junction, and then continue straight ahead. Fork left at the war memorial into Pound Lane, which is signed to Bransgore. Cycle past the Forest Teahouse and cider shop, then follow the lane out over the heath until you get to Burbush Hill.

2 Fork left just before the old railway bridge, following the waymarked off-road cycle track through the Forestry Commission's car park and down on to the old railway line. The Castleman Trail sets out from a lovely sandy cutting, which is smothered with brilliant purple heather in late summer. Soon the old line emerges from the cutting

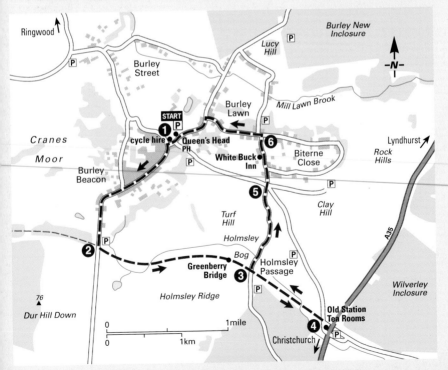

onto a low embankment, with good views out over the boggy heath. You'll often see horse-riders in the area and birders should look out for green woodpeckers, as well as for lapwings, curlews and redshanks, which nest on the heath in early summer. The trail rises briefly to the broken brickwork of Greenberry Bridge, which survived the closure of the railway, only to be demolished in 1995 when it became unsafe. Continue to the low wooden barriers that guard the minor road crossing at Holmsley Passage, where you can still see short sections of the original railway lines that are embedded in the road.

3 If you wish, you can shorten the ride by turning left here. To complete the full route, cross the road and continue along the old railway line. The trail becomes more shaded as it runs perfectly straight through an avenue of young oak trees. The track crosses two small bridges that herald the approach to Holmsley Station. Look out for the old brick platform on your right before dismounting at the wooden gate that marks the end of the cycle track.

4 Beyond the gate and across the road, the Old Station Tea Rooms are well worth a visit for morning coffee, tasty home-cooked lunches and delicious cream teas. There's a pleasant garden, as well as a gift shop where you can buy a souvenir of your visit to this unusual refreshment stop. Turn here and retrace your outward route to Holmsley Passage (Point 3). Turn right on to the quiet lane. Follow the lane up the hill and then stop at the 5-way junction.

5 Cross straight over towards Burley Lawn and zig-zag left, then right, past The White Buck Inn into Bennetts Lane.

6 Bear left when you reach the next junction leading into Beechwood Lane and keep straight on through Lester Square until you reach a T-junction. Turn left here towards Burley, and continue past the little brick-built Church of St John the Baptist for the final 400yds (366m) back to the car park.

Route facts

DISTANCE/TIME 6 miles (9.7km) 1h

MAP OS Explorer OL22 New Forest

START Public car park, (fee) Burley, grid ref: SU 211030

TRACKS Busy village centre, quiet lanes and an old railway route

GETTING TO THE START
Burley village is on a minor road southeast of Ringwood, between the A31 and the A35. Leave the A31 at Picket Post, 1 mile (1.6km) east of Ringwood, and follow the signposted route through Burley Street to Burley. Keep left at the war memorial in the centre of the village, and you'll find The Queens Head immediately on your left, with the public car park entrance just beyond the pub's own car park.

THE PUB The Queens Head, The Cross, Burley, Ringwood. Tel: 01425 403423

❶ Burley's streets get busy at weekends and during holiday periods. Good traffic sense required.

CHRISTCHURCH MAP REF SZ1892

This ancient town lies on the south coast where the rivers Stour and Avon pour their waters into the bay. At the time of the Domesday survey there were a mere 21 houses here, and it was then named Twynham. The church was started later in the 11th century, and became an Agustinian priory around 1150. Today all that remains is the Priory Church, which looms gold above the town, and is well worth exploring inside for its carvings in both stone and wood. Look out for the Norman turret in the north transept, and the superb carving of the Salisbury Chantry. Nearby Place Mill, mentioned in the Domesday Book, was used for fulling (cleaning and thickening cloth) and corn grinding until 1808, and now has displays of old milling items, with an art and crafts gallery upstairs.

One of Christchurch town's most unusual sights is its surviving ducking stool, reached via a flagged alleyway beside the Olde George Inn – a wooden stool on the end of a pole which can be swung out into the chilly millstream, in a scolds' punishment revived with good humour in 1986. The town's Red House Museum is a collection of local and natural history, housed in an appealing old Georgian house with a lovely garden.

Across the wide estuary, the pastel coloured nostalgic beach huts in rows on Mudeford's sandy peninsula are a cheerful throwback to childhood bucket-and-spade holidays of the early 20th century. This windswept peninsula has an archaeological record dating back 12,500 years, when Stone Age hunter-gatherers left the remains of a campsite on its outer, seaward edge. Some 10,500 years later, Iron Age folk had settled here and built up a good trading port on the inner shore, where Barn Field stands today. The great Double Dikes date from this period, built to shelter a village of timber-framed dwellings.

Barn Field itself has remained untouched by farming improvements since the Romans left in around AD 410 – a rare status jealously protected by conservationists. It's an area of low, acid grassland gripping onto thin soil over gravel and sand, maintained down the centuries by the salt-laden winds and the sharp teeth of the rabbit population. Decimation of the rabbits in the 1950s by myxomatosis allowed gorse and bramble to gain a hold, but a recent programme of scrub clearance and controlled grazing by cattle, managed by English Nature, has done much to restore the original balance. Today it is an important site for ground-nesting birds such as the skylark and meadow pipit, and adorned with heath bedstraw, autumn hawkbit and harebell.

ELING MAP REF SU3612

The Saxon village of Eling, on a little tidal creek off Southampton Water, was a shipbuilding village until the end of the 19th century. Before that it was a small port from where Henry I is said to have sailed to Normandy in 1130.

The creek, a sheltered little harbour for sailing craft, is crossed by a fast causeway with sluice gates to hold back the high tides and, in the little building on the northern shore, the power of Southampton Water's famous double

tides is harnessed and used to produce wholemeal flour. Eling Tide Mill is one of the few remaining tide mills regularly milling pure stoneground flour. The Domesday Book of 1086 records a mill here, but the present building dates from the 18th century. It was restored in 1980 and milling demonstrations are given, depending on the tides. You can learn more about Eling and neighbouring Totton in the heritage centre by the mill.

The causeway across the creek at Eling carries the only remaining toll road in Hampshire, which has been in operation since at least 1418.

EXBURY MAP REF SU4300

This pleasant estate village nestling on the Beaulieu River is famed for the magnificent rhododendron gardens at Exbury House. They were the creation of banker Lionel de Rothschild, whose passion was gardening – and he gardened on a magnificent scale. Rothschild started here in the 1920s,

with 600 acres (243ha) of wooded slopes overlooking the peaceful river, which he split into 250 acres (101ha) of gardens and 350 acres (142ha) of arboretum. He imported more than 1,000 varieties of rhododendron, then created 452 more by careful crossing. The mild climate of the Beaulieu River valley ensures a long flowering season, with breathtaking displays between April and June. Camellias, azaleas and magnolias contribute a great deal to the glory of an Exbury spring. Other 'gardens' on the site include a daffodil meadow, rock garden, rose garden, herbaceous garden and water garden. A miniature steam railway offers a 20-minute tour of the Summer Lane Garden, leading to the American Garden. Dogs on a short lead are welcome.

FORDINGBRIDGE
MAP REF SU1514

Fordingbridge stands at a shallow point on the River Avon, and is known as the northern gateway of the New Forest. It grew up around the light industries of pottery, brick-making and canvas sailcloth weaving, and has roots that date back to the Domesday survey and beyond. Branksome China, located on Shaftesbury Street, continues the old tradition of porcelain manufacture and hand painting, offering tours and a shop.

The town's elegant 14th-century bridge has seven arches, so solid in their stonework that they were drilled only with great difficulty during the Second World War by Royal Engineers, who were inserting explosives ready to blow the bridge up in the event of enemy invasion.

Visit

SOLDIER BROTHERS' MEMORIAL

In Exbury's Church of St Catherine is a fine bronze memorial by Cecil Thomas to John and Alfred Forster, brothers who were killed in the First World War. It shows a soldier's effigy lying on a tomb, and is impressively lifelike, down to the folds in the greatcoat and the lacing-up of the boots. The young sculptor was wounded in the war, and while in hospital met and befriended Lt Alfred Forster of the Royal Scots Greys, who later died of his wounds. After the war, Lord and Lady Forster commissioned Thomas to design a memorial to Alfred and his brother.

Despite the destruction of much of the old town by fire in 1702, there are around 70 listed buildings scattered through Fordingbridge, and a town walk takes you past many of the best. St Mary's Church is notable for the fine 15th-century carved roof in the north chancel chapel, and for its Miracle Stone on the outer wall of the north chapel. The Fordingbridge Museum includes an exhibition about the artist Augustus John, as well as artefacts to illustrate tales of smuggling in the town and many other curiosities.

South of the town off the A338, at South Gorley, Hockey's Farm is an open-air farming museum, with interesting fossil displays, a deer park, and a farm shop well stocked with home-produced beef and lamb, sausages, cakes and home-cured bacon.

FRITHAM MAP REF SU2314

The isolated rural hamlet of Fritham lies to the north of the A31. The plains to the south were used as an airfield during the Second World War, and to the north you'll find the lonely settlement, perhaps founded by squatters, known as Nomansland. The village inn, the Royal Oak, is a small traditional country pub, with few frills. Snug under its thatched roof, it is a reminder of a simple age when pigs snuffled in the woods, each home had a cow or two and some hens, services in the tiny tin chapel were held twice on Sundays attended by all, and the main road out was a grassy track.

Between 1863 and 1921, Fritham's fortunes changed and the village thrived as the base for an extensive gunpowder

■ Insight

ROYAL HUNTING GROUND

William the Conqueror created the New Forest as a preserve for deer, regarded from early times as the true sporting beasts of kings. Forest Law was severe and enforced to maintain the best possible environment for the 'beasts of the chase'. Today there are five species of deer in the forest, of which the most numerous are fallow deer. They are managed by the New Forest keepers, employed by the Forestry Commission. Of all the deer in the forest, the white buck, a rare albino form, was the most favoured. Legend has it that Henry VIII and his courtiers once chased a white buck quite a way through the forest towards Ringwood, and that he spared its life at the request of the ladies. Today the 'White Hart' appears on many an inn sign.

factory. The factory made use of locally produced charcoal and water from a chalybeate spring, still known as Irons Well. After the factory closed down, Fritham returned to a quieter existence.

At Canterton Glen, to the southeast of Fritham, lies the Rufus Stone, a small memorial marking the place where King William II (known as William Rufus), met his untimely death in 1100. King William loved hunting, and was killed by an arrow supposedly intended for a deer. The Rufus Stone is said to mark the spot, but some say it was much nearer Bolderwood, or Stoney Cross, or Fritham itself. Some question whether the King's death was an accident. Whatever the truth, his brother Henry rode straight to Winchester to be proclaimed king, while William's body was carried there on the cart of a charcoal burner.

A Forest Walk from Fritham

A walk from a hidden hamlet and the site of a former gunpowder factory, through woodland and open heathland. As you make your way through the peaceful mixed woodlands, look out for nests of wood ants beside the tracks, the mounds will be feverish with activity on dry warm days, and listen for the distinctive 'yaffle' of the green woodpecker, a common forest bird that feeds on the wood ants.

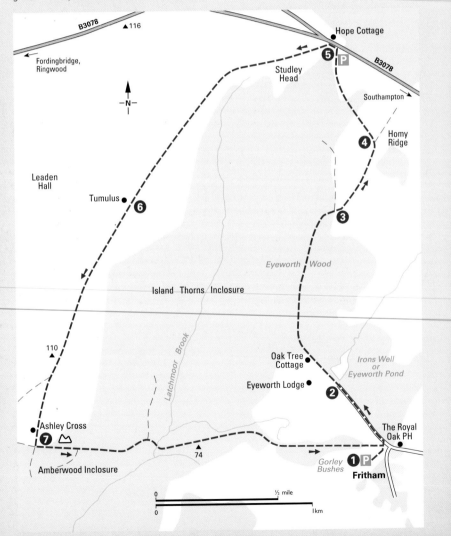

Route Directions

1 Turn left out of the car park and head downhill, along the road.

2 Keep ahead at the foot of the hill, leaving Eyeworth Pond on your right, and follow the short gravel track to a low wooden barrier at Oak Tree Cottage. Leave the barrier on your left, take the narrow path that heads north into Eyeworth Wood, and follow it for 0.5 mile (800m).

3 At length, the path leads on to a tree-studded heath, with far-reaching views. Continue for a further 550yds (503m) across Homy Ridge, as far as a stocky Scots pine tree at the edge of a small wood on your right.

4 The path divides here. Take the left-hand fork, and walk through the shallow valley to the car park at Telegraph Hill.

5 Turn left beside the B3078 for 20yds (18m), before turning left again on to the gravel track directly opposite Hope Cottage. The track bears left soon after passing a small, seasonal pond at Studley Head. After 250yds (229m), the path dives briefly beneath holly and oak trees before breaking back out on to the heath.

6 Continue past a deep pool on your right, just a few paces beyond the low mound of a tumulus. Follow the track south towards Amberwood Inclosure, ignoring the path that branches off to your right near Ashley Bottom. A little further on, look for the small brick shelter located on your right.

7 Turn left at a waymarked junction with the cycle track on the edge of Amberwood Inclosure, and dive steeply down the well-made gravel track into the woods. Ignore all turnings, and follow the waymarked route through the forest and over the Latchmoor Brook. The trees gradually drop behind as the cycle track winds its way up through Gorley Bushes, and there are glimpses of Eyeworth Lodge away to your left. A steady climb brings you to the green at Fritham. Turn right to return to the car park.

Route facts

DISTANCE/TIME
5.5 miles (8.8km) 3h

MAP OS OL22 New Forest

START Forestry Commission car park beyond Royal Oak pub, grid ref: SU 230141

TRACKS Gravel forest tracks, heathland and woodland paths

GETTING TO THE START
Fritham lies just off the A31 between Ringwood and Southampton, with easy access from the M27. At Stoney Cross turn off the A31 towards Fritham. After 2km (1.25 miles) take the second left, entering the village, then turn left again, following through the village until you reach the car park on your left.

THE PUB The Royal Oak, Fritham. Tel: 02380 812606

❶ Getting lost in the New Forest is deceptively easy so make sure you carry the necessary maps and guide information with you.

A Circuit around Linwood

This relatively remote ride offers a good chance of some peace and quiet, and the opportunity to see the New Forest at its best. You'll follow the waymarked Forestry Commission off-road cycle tracks deep into the heart of the forest for the majority of the ride, with two short sections on tarred roads where you will need to watch out for the occasional car. There are opportunities for birdwatching or, alternatively, for studying other local wildlife as you go through a variety of terrain. You are highly likely to see deer along this trail, especially if you come here early in the morning or at around dusk – go quietly for the best chance of seeing these timid woodland residents in their natural habitat.

Route Directions

1 Turn right out of the car park and continue straight on, passing the end of the gravel track that leads up to The High Corner Inn.

2 At Woodford Bottom bear left at the wooden barrier on your right and pass the ford across the Dockens Water stream, also on your right.

Keep to the waymarked cycle route as it closely follows the gravelled track that winds across the open heath, past a few scattered houses and the

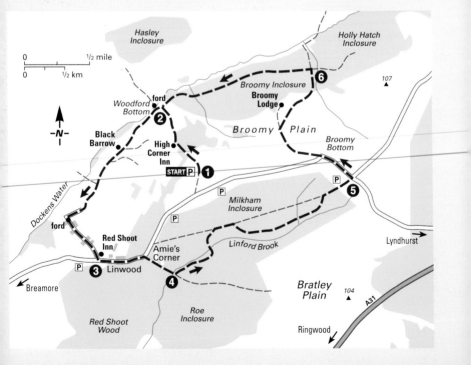

tree-capped mound of Black Barrow. A few smaller tracks lead off to left and right, but the main gravelled trail is easy enough to follow. Keep straight on as a similar track leads in from your left near the thatched Bogmyrtle Cottage, until you join a tarred lane. Almost at once the lane turns sharp left through a tiny ford and climbs gently up to the road junction at The Red Shoot Inn.

3 Turn left opposite the post-box, still following the waymarked cycle route, and continue to climb until the road levels off and swings to the left at Amie's Corner. Fork right here, sticking with the waymarked cycle route as it joins a gravelled forest track. The trail dives into Milkham Inclosure through wooden gates beside an attractive whitewashed cottage, then drops to a bridge over the Linford Brook.

4 A few yards further on turn left at the numbered waymark post 5, then follow the track as it winds through open mixed woodland and then re-crosses the Linford Brook. Continue as the track bears right at the next waymark post, then right again in front of a pair of wooden gates where you enter an area of

mainly coniferous woodland. Another pair of wooden gates punctuates your progress to the top of the hill, where further gates lead you out into the Forestry Commission's Milkham car park. Go through here, cross the car park, and stop at the road junction.

5 Turn left towards Linwood and follow the narrow tarred lane for 500yds (457m) until it bears away to the left. Fork right here on to the waymarked cycle trail that follows the gravel track towards Broomy Lodge and Holly Hatch. Here your route crosses the high heathland plateau of Broomy Plain. This is a good spot to see Dartford warblers, meadow pipits and stonechats, and you'll also enjoy good long views towards Cranborne Chase and the Wiltshire Downs. Bear right at the next fork and then follow the trail down into Holly Hatch Inclosure.

6 At the foot of the hill, numbered waymark post 3 stands at the forest cross-roads. Turn left here, on to a lovely tree-shaded track with soft green verges that leads you through the oak woods. Two pairs of wooden gates mark your progress through the inclosure, and at length the oaks give way to conifers.

Route facts

DISTANCE/TIME 7 miles (11.3km) 1h45

MAP OS Outdoor Leisure OL22 New Forest

START Spring Bushes car park, Linwood, grid ref: SU 196107

CYCLE HIRE The Railway Station, Brockenhurst. Tel: 01590 622627

TRACKS Gravelled forest tracks, two short sections on rural lanes

GETTING TO THE START Linwood is a village on a minor road northeast of Ringwood. Spring Bushes car park is on the road that runs west from Emery Down, near Lyndhurst, to Rockford, just north of Ringwood.

THE PUB The High Corner Inn, Linwood. Tel: 01425 473973

❶ Moderate hills, some uneven and stony tracks. Suitable for older children, some off-road riding experience useful.

Follow the waymarked trail until you rejoin your outward route at a low wooden barrier. Turn left here, and climb the short hill back to The High Corner Inn.

LYMINGTON MAP REF SZ3295

Lymington is a busy sailing town at the mouth of the Lymington River. It received its charter in 1200 and became a free port, flourishing as the closest mainland harbour to the Isle of Wight, to which ferries still run. In the Middle Ages Lymington rivalled Southampton as a major port – and the numerous creeks around here were much frequented by smugglers well into the 18th century. Today the tidal salt marshes stretch for 10 miles (16km), and are protected as a national nature reserve.

For many years the town's prosperity depended on the production of salt, but sadly this trade eventually died out and Lymington briefly became a fashionable bathing place. By the end of the 19th century it had really developed as a sailing centre, and today the town has an excellent yacht basin and is the headquarters of two sailing clubs. There is boat building too and, as with many ports, it is famed for its inns – reputedly there were once 45.

The wide Georgian and Victorian High Street, which climbs the hill from the quay to the church, bursts into life on Saturdays when there is a vibrant 700-year-old market, with a great variety of stalls laid out along both sides of the street. Enjoy the view from the hilltop back down across the river, then take a look at the Church of St Thomas, which looks 18th century, with its jaunty white cupola and galleried interior, but is actually medieval. The town's St Barbe Museum is dedicated to the history of the New Forest coast, including hands-on displays for children, while its art gallery offers an ever changing range of exhibitions of world-class artworks.

To the north of Lymington is lovely Spinners, a beautiful woodland garden showing rhododendrons, magnolias, Japanese maples and much more. To the south, on Hurst Spit, stands Hurst Castle, one of Henry VIII's defences and part of the modern coastal artillery defences until 1956.

LYNDHURST MAP REF SU3008

The 'Capital of the New Forest' is quite a sizeable town, and is the only one located within the historical confines of the forest. It was formerly designated the New Forest's administrative centre in 1079 by William I, and it continues to be the official seat of the ancient Court of Verderers whose aim is to protect the rights of the commoners. The Court Room and the Forestry Commission offices are both housed in the beautiful 17th-century Queen's House, and the Verderers meet here every two months. All New Forest animals are under their jurisdiction, while the patrolling of the forest is in the hands of four 'Agisters' – a medieval word meaning 'collector'. The Forestry Commission manages the woodland of the New Forest.

Lyndhurst is a town of narrow streets leading off the main High Street, which snarls up with traffic during peak holiday times. It is full of tourist shops and eating places, with Victorian and Edwardian architecture to admire. The church, on the site of two earlier ones, dominates the High Street with its 160-foot (49m) spire and dates from 1860. It contains windows by

■ Activity

THE HAMPSHIRE AVON

The River Avon rises to the east of Devizes and flows southwards for 48 miles (77km) to the English Channel at Christchurch. In its upper chalky reaches it is a noted trout stream, but where it flows into Hampshire past Breamore and Fordingbridge the acid soils of the New Forest change its nature and it becomes a river for coarse fishing. Below Ringwood it is renowned for salmon. The waymarked Avon Valley Path follows the river for 34 miles (54.5km) from Salisbury to Christchurch.

Burne-Jones and a fresco, *The Parable of the Virgins*, by Lord Leighton. In the village churchyard lies Mrs Hargreaves, who died in 1934. As the little Alice Liddell, she was the real inspiration for Lewis Carroll's *Alice in Wonderland*. The town is the home of the New Forest Visitor Centre and Museum.

Lyndhurst's central position makes it an ideal base for exploring the forest which still presses up close to the town's boundaries. To the west of Lyndhurst is the picturesque thatched hamlet of Swan Green, formerly the site of an important pony fair, and Emery Down, famed for its Portuguese fireplace, which stands alone in the open air. It was constructed of cobble stones on the site of a building that was occupied by Portuguese troops during the First World War, and serves as a memorial to them. The New Forest Reptile Centre, a conservation and education centre dedicated to rare native species, is near by. To the east is Bolton's Bench, an excellent starting point for walks over White Moor Heath.

In summer an open-topped City Sightseeing bus, with space for bicycles, runs every hour from Lyndhurst, and makes 13 stops at key points which include Lymington and Beaulieu.

MINSTEAD MAP REF SU2811

Minstead consists of clusters of cottages amid trees and pastures, centred on the inn and the church. The latter is of curious construction, having the outward appearance of an old house, all gables and dormers. This is the result of successive 'updates' by local builders who had little idea of ecclesiastical construction, reflecting the unhurried days when the forest turned in on itself and knew little of the world beyond. The interior has rows of box pews and a plethora of galleries. Sir Arthur Conan Doyle (1867–1930), whose most famous literary creation was the detective Sherlock Holmes, lies buried here.

To the northwest of the village lies Furzey Gardens, renowned among many botanists and horticulturists, comprising 8 acres (3ha) of informal planting, which includes azaleas, rhododendrons, ferns, heathers and Chilean fire trees. Within the garden are a thatched Tudor cottage, a crafts gallery and an art gallery.

RINGWOOD MAP REF SU1505

Ringwood is a venerable town on the River Avon, and anglers come from miles around for the coarse and salmon fishing of this reach. This busy centre has always been the New Forest's market town, with its modern buildings blending well with the Georgian houses and older cottages.

There is a good modern shopping centre, and the attractive High Street has traditional shops including fishing tackle suppliers and a gunsmith. The Ringwood Brewery has an outlet on Christchurch Road. In West Street stands Monmouth House, where the Duke of Monmouth was held after his defeat at Sedgemoor in 1685, before being sent to London for execution.

Learn more about the history of the area at the Ringwood Town & Country Experience, a heritage centre to the north of the A31, with reconstructed Victorian shop interiors, a fabulous carousel, and one of the bouncing bombs, developed nearby for the RAF 'Dambusters' in the Second World War. The Moors Valley Country Park at Ashley Heath offers walks and cycle trails, and other attractions, including a narrow-gauge steam railway.

To the south of Ringwood, at Crow, is Liberty's Owl, Raptor and Reptile Centre, named after a star attraction – an American bald eagle. There are lots of birds of prey, including eagles, hawks, owls and vultures, which take part in regular flying displays, and reptiles such as giant tortoises, snakes and lizards.

ROCKBOURNE MAP REF SU1118

The village of Rockbourne, on the high chalklands northwest of Fordingbridge, is one of Hampshire's prettiest villages, with thatched cottages dating back to Tudor and Georgian times nestling beside a stream in a valley bottom. On the downs above the village are the remains of three barrows: Grans, Knapp and Duck's Nest Long Barrow.

Rockbourne's real fame, however, rests on the Roman villa discovered to the south of the village by a farmer in 1942, when he was digging out a ferret. The villa was a large courtyard type of mansion, possibly part of an imperial estate, with more than 70 rooms, several bath suites, farm houses and work-shops. It was occupied from the mid-2nd century AD until the collapse of Roman rule in the early 5th century. Although much of it has been excavated it has to some extent been backfilled for its own protection, since the site is not under cover, but several mosaics may be seen as you walk around.

As well as the villa, there was a small settlement and a probable cattle enclosure on Rockbourne Down, while nearby Bokerley Dyke, a late Roman earthwork, acts as a local boundary. The museum attached to the villa has pottery, jewellery and elaborate iron work, a large coin hoard and two Roman milestones. Found in the fabric of the villa, where they had been re-used as building material, the milestones date from the reigns of Trajan Decius (AD 249–51) and Tetricus II (AD 272).

■ Insight

HORSE FLESH

To the northeast of Rockbourne lies the peaceful village of Whitsbury. It is home to the Whitsbury Manor Stud, one of the most successful horse breeding, training and racing stables in Britain. The open downland surrounding the village provides an ideal training ground for potential winners. Racehorses Desert Orchid and Rhyme and Reason were both bred here.

New Forest trails around Bank

Ancient oaks, towering conifers and historic inclosures (different areas of managed woodlands where young trees are protected from deer and ponies) are on the route. Soon after beginning the walk you'll pass the most famous and probably the oldest tree in the forest, the Knightwood Oak. It is thought to be at least 350 years old and owes its age to pollarding its limbs to encourage new branches for fuel.

Route Directions

1 Take the gravel path at the southern end of the car park (beyond the information post), parallel with the road.

In 100yds (91m) turn right just before a bench seat and descend to a gravel track. Cross straight over; then,

where the path curves left, keep ahead to reach a gate and the A35. Cross over the A35 (take care), go through

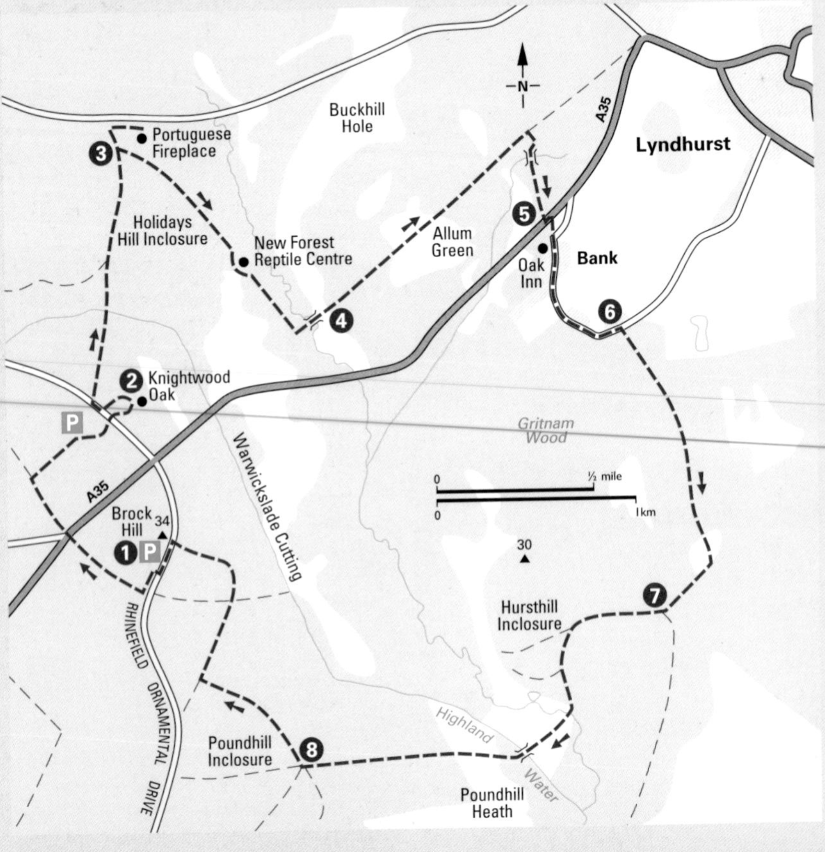

Buckhill Hole

—N—

A35

3 Portuguese Fireplace

Lyndhurst

Holidays Hill Inclosure

New Forest Reptile Centre

Allum Green

5

Oak Inn

Bank

4

6

2 Knightwood Oak

P

Gritnam Wood

A35

Brock Hill **34**

1 P

Warwickslade Cutting

0 ————— ½ mile

0 ————— 1km

30 ▲

RHINEFIELD ORNAMENTAL DRIVE

Hursthill Inclosure

7

Highland Water

Poundhill Inclosure **8**

Poundhill Heath

a gate and keep to the path, uphill to a junction. Turn right and follow the path to Knightwood Oak car park, then follow the sign to the Knightwood Oak itself.

2 Return towards the car park and bear right along the road. Turn right again after a few paces, on to a path into mixed woodland. Cross a stream and soon reach a gravel track. Bear right and keep to this trail, passing red marker posts, to a fork. Keep left to reach a gate and road. Turn right to view the Portuguese Fireplace.

3 Return through Holidays Hill Inclosure to the fork of tracks. Bear left and follow this to the New Forest Reptile Centre. Walk along the access drive past a cottage dated 1811 then, at a barrier on your left, drop down on to a path and follow it across a bridge.

4 Keep to the main path for 0.75 mile (1.2km), skirting the walls to Allum Green and several clearings, then gently climb through trees to a defined crossing of paths and turn right. Shortly, bear half right across a clearing and concrete footbridge, then continue through the woodland edge to an electricity pole. Bear right

for 20yds (18m), then left through a gate to the A35.

5 Turn left, then almost immediately right across the road to a gate. Walk ahead to a garden boundary and turn right, the narrow path leading to a lane in Bank. Turn right, pass the Oak Inn and walk through the hamlet.

6 Just beyond the cattle grid, turn right through a gate on to a gravelled track towards Brockenhurst. Follow this track for nearly a mile (1.6km) to a junction at a small green.

7 Fork right towards Brockenhurst, and enter Hursthill Inclosure at a gate. Drop down past a turning on the right, then climb again and bear left at a fork. Keep to the waymarked track as it drops past another turning on the right and leaves Hursthill Inclosure at a gate. Walk the long straight track to the bridge over Highland Water, and follow the track round to the right. Soon a gate leads the waymarked trail into Poundhill Inclosure, and another straight section brings you to a five-way junction at waymark post 24.

8 Turn right here. Ignore all turnings, and follow the track as it turns sharp right and

Route facts

DISTANCE/TIME
8 miles (12.9km) 4h

MAP OS Explorer OL22
New Forest

START Brock Hill Forestry
Commission car park,
grid ref: SU 266057

TRACKS Grass and gravel
forest tracks, heathland
paths, some roads

GETTING TO THE START
Look for signs to the
Rhinefield Ornamental
Drive, just off the A35
Lyndhurst-to-Christchurch
road, some 3 miles (4.8km)
southwest of Lyndhurst.
Parking is signposted on
the right, a short distance
off the A35.

THE PUB The Oak Inn,
Pinkney Lane, Bank.
Tel: 023 8028 2350

❶ Extreme caution needed
when crossing the busy A35
(twice). Blind bends on the
lane through Bank. Follow
directions carefully –
unsigned paths, tracks and
forest rides.

winds its way to a junction with the Ornamental Drive. Turn left for the last 100 yards (91m) back to the car park.

Around Roman Rockbourne

Through rolling fields and areas of dense woodland, this walk discovers Rockbourne, a gem of a place that has one of the prettiest village high streets in Hampshire and is also home to one of the most interesting Roman villa complexes in the country. You can stop here to see the remains of the villa, its heating system and beautiful mosaics. The walk route continues to the neighbouring village of Whitsbury, where foundations of another Roman building, containing a hypocaust and New Forest pottery dating back to the 2nd and 3rd century AD, were found overlaying earlier, Iron Age settlements on a hill-fort.

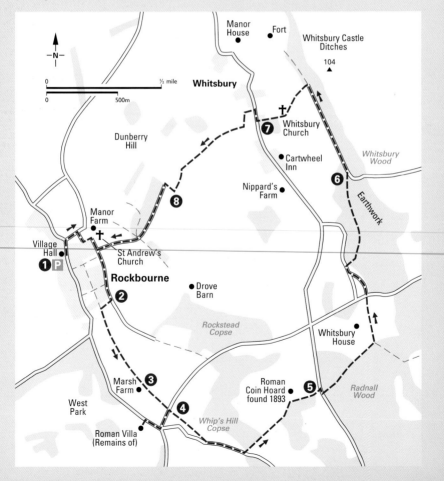

Route Directions

1 Turn left out of the village hall car park and shortly take the lane right towards Manor Farm. Turn right, signed to the church, and cross the gravel drive to a stepped path to St Andrew's Church. Continue along the right-hand edge of the churchyard to reach a junction of paths. Keep straight on behind houses, ignoring three paths right, then cross a stile and turn immediately right to go through a gate.

2 Follow the field-edge down to a junction of paths. Turn left and cross a stile to a gate, then cross a stile, go through a gate and along the field-edge. In the far corner of the field, zig-zag right and left over a stile and keep along the edge of a meadow to a stile. Pass in front of a thatched cottage to reach a gate and track, opposite Marsh Farm.

3 Bear left, then right through a gate and continue along the right-hand field-edge to a gate. Continue to another gate, then turn left along the field-edge, passing through a gate to reach a stile and lane. To visit the Roman Villa, turn right to a T-junction, and turn right, then left to the entrance. Retrace your steps.

4 Take the track opposite. Enter a copse, then at a junction of tracks, take the arrowed path left up a steep bank into a field. Follow the path parallel to the field-edge to reach a stile at the corner of a wood. Cross a track, and continue downhill inside the woodland edge to a lane.

5 Turn right, then left along a bridleway, and gently climb through Radnall Wood. At a junction bear left (follow the blue arrow) and pass behind Whitsbury House to a lane. Turn left, then right along a track between properties to a lane. Turn right, then bear off right (by a fingerpost) along the bridleway through Whitsbury Wood.

6 At a junction with a track, bear left and walk beside paddocks to a bungalow. Turn left along a track between paddocks towards Whitsbury church. Turn left at the T-junction and shortly enter the churchyard. Go through the gate opposite the church door and descend to the lane.

7 Turn left for the Cartwheel Inn, otherwise turn right, then left along a farm drive and keep ahead, bearing left, then right between paddocks, uphill to a gate. Turn left along the field-edge, and then head across the field to a track.

8 Turn right and follow the track left to a junction of tracks. Go through the gate opposite and then walk back to Rockbourne church. Retrace your steps back to the village hall.

Route facts

DISTANCE/TIME
4.5 miles (7.2km) 2h15

MAP OS Explorer OL22 New Forest

START Rockbourne village hall car park, grid ref: SU 113184

TRACKS Field paths, woodland bridleways and tracks, 9 stiles

GETTING TO THE START Take the A338 south from Salisbury. At Fordingbridge take the B3078 west through Sandleheath and follow the signs to Rockbourne village.

THE PUB The Rose & Thistle, Rockbourne. Tel: 01725 518236

■ TOURIST INFORMATION CENTRES

Fordingbridge
Kings Yard, Salisbury Street.
Tel: 01425 654560;
www.visitfordingbridge.com

Christchurch
49 High Street.
Tel: 01202 471780;
www.christchurchtourism.info

Lyndhurst
New Forest Visitor
Information Centre,
Main car park.
Tel: 023 8028 2269;
www.thenewforest.co.uk

■ PLACES OF INTEREST

Apple Court Garden & Nursery
Hordle Lane, Hordle,
Lymington. Tel: 01590 642130;
www.applecourt.com

Beaulieu: National Motor Museum
Palace House,
Beaulieu Abbey
Tel: 01590 612123;
www.beaulieu.co.uk

Bolderwood Deer Platform
Signed from Bolderwood car
park. Fallow deer fed here.
www.forestry.gov.uk/newforest

Branksome China
Fordingbridge.
Tel: 01425 652010;
www.branksomechina.co.uk

Breamore Manor House & Countryside Museum
Tel: 01725 512468;
www.breamorehouse.com

Buckler's Hard
Tel: 01590 616203;
www.bucklershard.co.uk

Calshot Fort (EH)
Tel: 02380 892023

Christchurch Priory Church
Quay Road, Christchurch.
Tel: 01202 485804;
www.christchurchpriory.org

Eling Tide Mill
The Toll Bridge, Eling, Totton.
Tel: 023 8086 9575;
www.elingtidemill.org.uk

Exbury Gardens & Steam Railway
Near Beaulieu.
Tel: 023 8089 1203;
www.exbury.co.uk

Fordingbridge Museum
King's Yard, Fordingbridge.
Tel: 01425 655222; www.
fordingbridgemuseum.co.uk

Furzey Gardens
Minstead.
Tel: 023 8081 2464;
www.furzey-gardens.org

Hockey's Farm
South Gorley.
Tel: 01425 652542. Free.

Hurst Castle
Hurst Point, by Keyhaven.
Tel: 01590 642344;
www.hurst-castle.co.uk
Accessible on foot, or
by boat from Keyhaven
every 30 minutes.

Moors Valley Country Park
Ashley Heath, Ringwood.
Tel: 01425 470721

New Forest Cider
Littlemead, Pound Lane,

Burley.
Tel: 01425 403589;
www.newforestcider.co.uk

New Forest Museum
Main car park, High Street,
Lyndhurst.
Tel: 023 8028 3444;
www.newforestcentre.org.uk

New Forest Reptile Centre
Emery Down.
Tel: 023 8028 3141;
www.forestry.gov.uk/newforest

Place Mill
Quay Road, Christchurch.
Tel: 01202 487626;
www.visitchristchurch.info

Red House Museum
Quay Road, Christchurch.
Tel: 01202 482860

Ringwood Brewery Store
138 Christchurch Road,
Ringwood.
Tel: 01425 471177;
www.ringwoodbrewery.co.uk

Rockbourne Roman Villa
Tel: 01725 518541;
www.hants.gov.uk/museum/
rockbourne

St Barbe Museum & Art Gallery
New Street, Lymington.
Tel: 01590 676969;
www.stbarbe-museum.org.uk

Sammy Miller Motorcycle Museum & Farm Trust
New Milton.
Tel: 01425 620777;
www.sammymiller.co.uk

Spinners Garden & Nursery
Boldre, by Lymington.
Tel: 01590 675488

■ FOR CHILDREN

Liberty's Owl, Raptor and Reptile Centre
Crow Lane, Crow.
Tel: 01425 476487;
www.libertyscentre.co.uk

Longdown Activity Farm
South of A35, near Ashurst.
Tel: 023 8029 3326;
www.longdownfarm.co.uk

New Forest Safaris
Burley Park, Burley.
Tel: 07801 345264;
www.newforestsafari.co.uk

New Forest Wildlife Park
Longdown, near Ashurst.
Tel: 023 8029 2408;
www.newforestwildlifepark.
co.uk

Paultons Park
Ower, near Romsey.
Tel: 023 8081 4455;
www.paultonspark.co.uk

■ SHOPPING

Farmers' Markets
Held in towns throughout the
New Forest. Markets take
place on alternate Sundays
in Beaulieu, Lymington,
Lyndhurst and Fordingbridge.
Tel: 023 8028 5185; www.
forestfriendlyfarming.org.uk.

Christchurch Market
High Street, every Mon.

Lyburn Farmhouse Cheesemakers
Lyburn Farm, Landford,
Wiltshire.
Tel: 01794 390451;
www.lyburncheese.co.uk

■ SPORTS & ACTIVITIES

Go Ape!
Moors Valley Country Park,
Horton Road, Ashley Heath.
Tel: 0870 458 9063;
www.goape.co.uk
High-wire forest adventure.

BOATING

Beaulieu River cruises
From Buckler's Hard, 3 miles
(4.8km) south of Beaulieu.

Liquid Logistics
Tel: 01590 612377;
www.liquidlogistics.co.uk
Canoeing and kayaking.

Mudeford Ferry
Mudeford Quay.
Tel: 01202 488662;
www.mudefordferry.co.uk

CYCLE HIRE

AA Bike Hire
Fernglen, Gosport Lane,
Lyndhurst.
Tel: 023 8028 3349;
www. aabikehirenewforest.
co.uk

Country Lanes Cycle Centre
The Railway Station,
Brockenhurst.
Tel: 01590 622627;
www.countrylanes.co.uk

Cycle Xperience Bike Hire
Island Shop, 2–4 Brookly
Road, Brockenhurst.
Tel: 01590 624204;
www.cyclex.co.uk

Forest Leisure Cycling
Burley.
Tel: 01425 403584;
www.forestleisurecycling.co.uk

FISHING

Orchard Lakes
New Lane Orchard, New
Lane, Bashley, New Milton.
Tel: 01425 612404
Carp, tench, chub, bream,
roach and rudd.

Everton Grange Lake
Braxton Farm, Lymore Lane,
Milford-on-Sea, Lymington.
Tel: 01590 644499
Carp, chub and tench.

RIDING

Burley-Villa School of Riding
Bashley Common Road,
New Milton.
Tel: 01425 610278;
www.burleyvilla.co.uk

WALKING

Avon Valley Path
A 34-mile (55km) path from
Christchurch to Salisbury
Cathedral.

Castleman Trailway
A 16-mile (26km) trail
between Upton and
Ringwood.

■ ANNUAL EVENTS & CUSTOMS

Beaulieu
Boat Jumble, Apr.
Auto Jumble, Sep.
Fireworks, end Oct.

Brockenhurst
New Forest Show, last week
Jul at New Park.
www.newforestshow.co.uk

Mudeford
Lifeboat Funday, end Jul
on Mudeford Quay.

KING WILLIAM
THE SECOND,
SURNAMED RUFUS
BEING SLAIN,
AS BEFORE RELATED,
WAS LAID IN A
CART, BELONGING
TO ONE PURKIS,
AND DRAWN FROM
HENCE, TO
WINCHESTER, AND
BURIED IN THE
CATHEDRAL CHURCH,
OF THAT CITY.

Tea Rooms

The Buttery
19–20 High Street,
Lymington SO41 9AD
Tel: 01590 672870;
www.thebuttery.org
A well-established and
deservedly popular restaurant
and tea room, the Buttery
serves speciality coffees and
teas, clotted cream teas, and
a great selection of tasty
cakes – all handmade on the
premises. You can also get
light lunches here, and even
a full English breakfast.

The Buttery at the Brock & Bruin
25 Brookley Road,
Brockenhurst SO42 7RB
Tel: 01590 622958
Home-made cakes and
cream teas are top treats
at this restaurant and tea
room. Light lunches are also
served daily.

Montagu Arms Hotel
Palace Lane,
Beaulieu SO42 7ZL
Tel: 01590 612324; www.
montaguarmshotel.co.uk
An hospitable, 16th-century
inn nestling in the pretty
hamlet of Beaulieu, the
Montagu Arms offers finger
sandwiches, loaf cakes,
scones, cream tea fancies,
and shortbread. In season,
you can enjoy locally grown
strawberries served with your
afternoon tea.

Tasty Pastries Bakery and Tea Room
16A High Street,
Lyndhurst SO43 7BD
Tel: 023 8028 3448
The perfect place to pause for
tea and cakes, or perhaps to
buy freshly baked pasties,
filled baguettes and
sandwiches for a picnic.

Pubs

The East End Arms
Main Road, East End,
near Lymington SO41 5SY
Tel: 01590 626223;
www.eastendarms.co.uk
A traditional New Forest pub
serving brasserie-style food
in the lounge bar, such as
Toulouse sausages and
toasted goats' cheese
baguettes. No food served
Sunday evening. Book in
advance for Sunday lunch.

The Filly Inn
Lymington Road, Setley,
Brockenhurst SO42 7UF
Tel: 01590 623449;
www.fillyinn.co.uk
The bar snacks at this cosy,
traditional pub include
baguettes and jacket
potatoes, and there is a wider
menu offering home-baked
pies and perhaps roast ribs in
barbecue sauce. Vegetarian
options include spinach and
mushroom lasagne and
sundried tomato and
asparagus risotto. Children
are welcome, and dogs
permitted too.

The Master Builders House Hotel
Bucklers Hard SO42 7XB
Tel: 01590 616297;
www.themasterbuilders.co.uk
Grassy areas in front of the
pub run down to the Beaulieu
River, making it a popular
spot, especially on summer
days. Fish pie and beef
bourguignon may appear on
the menu, with a good range
of light snacks. Beers include
Greene King IPA.

The Rose & Thistle
Rockbourne SP6 3NL
Tel: 01725 518236;
www.roseandthistle.co.uk
This postcard-perfect
thatched and whitewashed
pub has a rose arch and
flowers blooming around
the door. Fresh food is cooked
to order, from Welsh rarebit
and roast beef ploughman's
to smoked salmon tagliatelle.
There is more substantial
fare on the evening menu,
such as venison steak with
chestnut sauce, or chicken
with herby lentils. Beers
include Adnams Broadside
and Wadworth 6X.

Isle of Wight

INTRODUCTION

The Isle of Wight is the largest island off England's coast. It is separated from the mainland by the Solent and for many years was isolated and forgotten, until popularised in the mid-19th century by the arrival of Queen Victoria and Prince Albert, who built Osborne House here. This is an island of contrasts: the north facing the mainland; the southwest, including the famous Needles battered by Channel storms; and the southeast basking in a subtropical climate. The Isle of Wight has a timeless, old fashioned appeal which lingers on, born of its long separation from the mainland and an independent way of life; indefinable but nevertheless real, it helps to explain the island's perennial popularity.

6 Walk start point

3 Cycle start point

Fishbourne
Ryde
A3054
Seaview
B3330
Havenstreet
A3055
St Helens
Brading
Bembridge   Foreland
B3395
Culver Cliff
Apse
Heath   **Sandown**
Sandown
Bay
Shanklin
Dunnose
Ventnor

Gosport
Portsmouth
Gilkicker Point

VENTNOR

YARMOUTH

Unmissable attractions

Join the thousands of boat enthusiasts at Cowes during the island's world-famous sailing regatta held in August...photograph Godshill's chocolate-box pretty, stone and thatched cottages...walk the 15th-century ramparts of Carisbrooke Castle...soak up the atmosphere at stunning Osborne House, Queen Victoria's favourite residence and place of her death...enjoy the traditional seaside amusements and attractions at Sandown...admire the bay views and the quintessentially English beach huts that stand guard on the beach at Shanklin...go to Ventnor, famous in the 19th century for its allegedly curative waters...visit 13th-century Calbourne Mill, still in use today.

1 Cowes
The town is the scene of the annual Cowes Week regatta when the marina bustles with yachts, sailors and sightseers.

2 Carisbrooke Castle
This 11th-century castle has had a long and varied history but is most well known as a place of imprisonment for Charles I.

3 Freshwater Bay
Popular with walkers, the cove here was well known to Alfred, Lord Tennyson, whose house above the cliffs looked out to sea.

4 Shanklin Chine
Shanklin is home to more than 150 varieties of plants. You will see many of them on a walk through the chine.

5 The Needles
On the hill above the Needles is the 19th-century Needles Battery. The battery formed a part of the coastal defences during both world wars.

ALUM BAY MAP REF SZ3185

The soaring, spikey chalk outcrops of the Needles are the Isle of Wight's most famous landmark, stretching out to the west and clearly visible from the Dorset coast. Standing around 500 feet (150m) high, they sport a red-and-white striped lighthouse, topped by a small helicopter landing platform, which is best seen via boat trips from Alum Bay.

Set at right angles to the chalk, the cliffs at Alum Bay produce the island's most unusual souvenirs: a range of clear glass novelty items that display the distinctive 12 shades of sand. The colours range from pink and gold to orange and brown, and are all found naturally in the cliffs here. Within the Needles Park complex, you'll find a specialist glass shop and a sweet shop.

The sandstone strata of the cliffs are vertical, and were formed some 50 million years ago. You can view them from a spectacular chairlift ride down the cliffs to the beach at the bottom.

Activity

THE TENNYSON TRAIL

This 14-mile (21km) trail starts from Carisbrooke and heads southwest up on to Bowcombe Down, then west past many prehistoric tumuli, and into Brighstone Forest, with views over Brighstone Bay. It then heads back up and over onto Mottistone Down and Brook Down before a long descent past the golf course on Afton Down into Freshwater Bay, where it follows the coast path above the cliff. This is Tennyson Down, with a 38-foot (11.5m) monument to the poet at the high point. The path then drops into Alum Bay.

On the cliff edge is a monument to the noted Italian physicist and inventor, Marconi, who set up a pioneering wireless and telegraph station here at the end of the 19th century.

The Needles Old Battery at Totland is a gun battery and fort with wonderful views over the Needles to the Dorset coast. It was built in 1863 as part of the defences for the large naval base at Portsmouth. Exhibitions tell the story of the fort during the two world wars, and the headland's past as a secret base for rocket testing. Note that access is on foot, and it's a 15-minute walk across the downs from the Alum Bay car park.

BEMBRIDGE MAP REF SZ6588

Bembridge, on the island's eastern tip, was a remote little fishing village in a sheltered haven leading to Brading Quay until the Brading Harbour Improvement and Railway Company set out to reclaim the upper reaches of the haven. They created a deep-water port here, building an embankment between Bembridge and St Helens in 1878 to carry both road and rail. But Bembridge's days as a port were already numbered, and the ferry service to the mainland lasted only until 1888, because the new harbour suffered from silting, although the railway survived until the 20th century.

Today Bembridge is a popular sailing centre and a quiet resort with pleasant walks inland over the reclaimed haven, now marshy meadows, to Brading. At Bembridge Point is the famous Pilot Boat Inn, built in the shape of a boat, and the lifeboat station near by houses displays on its modern, unsinkable craft.

Bembridge Down is crowned by Fort Bembridge (1862–67), the main Victorian fort for the southern Isle of Wight, and offshore, four forts are still visible – the remains of the Victorian defences for Spithead. Bembridge Windmill, half a mile (1km) to the south, dates from 1700 and has its original wooden machinery.

BRADING MAP REF SZ6187

In Roman times Bembridge Down was a separate island and Brading faced it across a tidal channel. In about AD 300 the Romans built a villa here, one of the best in Britain with fabulous mosaics, and it remained occupied until the 5th century. Nowadays a vineyard clothes the slopes near the villa, continuing a tradition begun in Roman times. In 1338 an embankment was built at Yar Bridge, creating a harbour in order to connect Bembridge Down with the rest of the Isle of Wight. Brading became an important port, but the harbour here, too, suffered from increased silting. It was reclaimed in 1878–80 and is now an area of marshy meadows, a favourite breeding ground for birds.

As well as the vineyard and Roman Villa, Brading is also home to The Lilliput Antique Doll & Toy Museum, which has more than 2,000 exhibits and will delight children and adults alike. In the town centre, look out for the whipping post and stocks outside the Old Town Hall. For walkers, nearby Brading and Arreton Downs are great places for a walk, with breathtaking sea views. The Church of St Mary, the oldest church on the island, is believed to mark the spot where St Wilfred converted the Isle of Wight to Christianity, and a chapel contains tombs of the Oglander family, important in affairs of the island for 800 years.

To the northwest of Brading is Nunwell House, a 17th-century mansion and seat of the Oglanders from the Norman conquest till 1980. Charles I spent his last night on the island here. The house is furnished and the gardens include a walled garden.

CALBOURNE MAP REF SZ4287

Calbourne is tucked under the downs in the west of the island, an unspoiled little place with a village green, a Norman and a 13th-century church, and pretty stone cottages. The best of these are in Barrington Row, and these low thatched cottages at the back of the village face the diminutive Caul Burn. The stream once powered five watermills. The last surviving, Calbourne Mill, first mentioned in 1299, is still in working order, and there is an attached rural life museum with interesting old appliances. West of Calbourne, Chessell Pottery is housed in a large old barn. To the east is historic Swainstone House, now a hotel, renovated after being burned out in an air raid in 1941. It was named after Swein, the 8th- to 9th-century Danish leader, and later belonged to the Bishop of Winchester. The attached 13th-century chapel survived intact.

To the south of Calbourne, Mottistone Manor Garden has splendid views, and is known for its herbaceous borders and grassy terraces, planted with fruit trees. There are lots of walking trails through the surrounding estate.

CARISBROOKE CASTLE

CARISBROOKE MAP REF SZ4888

Carisbrooke, once the capital of the Isle of Wight, is inland above the Medina River to the west of the modern capital, Newport, and is overlooked by its castle, one of England's most impressive. High Street is pleasant, and narrow Castle Street leads up from an old ford and a streamside footpath to get to the castle. St Mary's Church, with its lofty 15th-century tower, was the church of a priory dissolved as long ago as 1415.

Carisbrooke Castle is a big, well-preserved Norman fortress built high on an artificial mound. The oldest parts are the keep and the surviving sections of curtain walls, which were constructed in the 12th century and strengthened at the end of the 16th century. A head for heights is needed to walk the ramparts, but you will be rewarded with excellent views of the interior of the castle and the surrounding countryside. A great attraction is the well, 161 feet (49m) deep, with a 16th-century wheel to draw up the water in buckets. It is worked today by donkeys – learn more at the Donkey Centre. The castle also houses the fascinating Isle of Wight Museum.

COWES MAP REF SZ4996

Cowes, on the island's northern tip, is divided by the River Medina. On the west bank is the sailing capital of Britain, on the east is a residential and industrial area, where high-speed ships, flying boats and seaplanes were built during World War II, and the Hovercraft was developed. Beyond all this lies the tranquillity of Osborne House, Queen Victoria's favourite residence.

West Cowes, home of the Royal Yacht Squadron, has an attractive winding High Street and a good array of shops. You can see ships and boats of all sorts from the Victoria Parade. The inaugural Cowes Regatta took place between naval vessels in 1776, and the yacht club was founded in 1815. In 1856 Cowes Castle became the Squadron's headquarters, and the 22 brass guns from the *Royal Adelaide*, King William IV's yacht, were positioned in front of the castle to start races and salute victorious yachts – as they still do. There have always been Royal yachtsmen – including Edward VII, George IV, George V, Prince Philip and Prince Edward – and during Cowes Week in August the little town is alive with the great and the good of the yachting fraternity.

Cowes has a Maritime Museum, a military history museum, and the Sir Max Aitken Museum, which has a display of nautical instruments, paintings and artefacts.

FRESHWATER MAP REF SZ3487

The southwest tip of the Isle of Wight which ends in the jagged sea-girt chalk pinnacles of The Needles is known as the Freshwater Peninsula. The village of Freshwater itself is large and bustling, and was made famous by poet Alfred, Lord Tennyson who came to reside at Farringford – now a hotel – in 1853, soon after he was proclaimed Poet Laureate. He lived there until 1867 when inquisitive visitors, wishing to see the famous man as he walked on the down in cloak and broad-brimmed hat, drove him to his refuge on the Surrey/Sussex border.

Insight

RUINED SHELL

Appuldurcombe House, once Hampshire's finest English baroque building, is now a ruined shell, standing in wooded country to the south amid beautiful grounds landscaped by 'Capability' Brown. The mansion was built in 1710 for Sir Robert Worsley, who is commemorated with an obelisk on the nearby down. The house has been uninhabitable since it was bombed in 1943, during World War II.

Freshwater has now spread south down the western Yar valley towards Freshwater Bay. The famous portrait photographer Julia Margaret Cameron settled here in the 1860s, and her home, Dimbola Lodge, on Terrace Lane, is now a museum to her work.

GODSHILL MAP REF SZ5383

Nestling prettily beneath its beautiful 15th-century church tower, this little village of stone-built, thatched cottages is the most visited and photographed place on the island. Attractions include the interesting model of Godshill village and the Nostalgia Toy Museum, and the Old Smithy and Gardens. Godshill is very popular, so come early in the morning to avoid the coaches and the crowds or in the evening after they have gone.

However, one peaceful haven here is the lovely church, which is almost 1,000 years old and contains a rare medieval wall painting, a painting of Daniel in the lions' den (attributed to Rubens), and some monuments to the Worsley family of Appuldurcombe. The nearby Owl and Falconry Centre offers flying displays.

NEWPORT MAP REF SZ5088

Newport, the capital of the Isle of Wight, is a venerable old market town on the River Medina. Its squares and narrow, twisting streets may hide the river from the view of the cursory visitor but boats still ply their trade at the rejuvenated quay. Here, too, you'll find the arts centre, housed in a large converted warehouse. The pleasant High Street has many attractive buildings, and is dominated by the Guildhall, with its fine Ionic portico market designed by John Nash, now home to the Museum of Island History. St Thomas' Church has a beautiful marble monument designed by Marochetti to Princess Elizabeth, the youngest daughter of Charles I, who died of a fever aged 14 while she was a prisoner in Carisbrooke Castle.

The town was founded in medieval times as the 'new port' for the old capital, Carisbrooke, yet, similarly to Carisbrooke, it can claim to have its roots in Roman times, since a Roman villa, dating from the 3rd century AD, was discovered here in 1926. The villa has been excavated and is now open to the public. Three of the public rooms have tessellated floors, and the largest also has a fireplace – this was an unusual feature in a Roman house. There is also a reconstructed Roman herb garden.

Just to the northwest of the town is Parkhurst Prison and further on you'll find Parkhurst Forest, the remaining glades and woodlands of a former royal hunting forest. This ancient woodland has been threaded by waymarked paths and is now one of the last remaining refuges of the red squirrel.

NEWTOWN MAP REF SZ4291

Newtown was originally founded in the 13th century on the island's northwest coast, and its grid-iron pattern can be recognised even today. Its large natural harbour was reputed to have anchorage for 50 ships, but continual silting reduced its size and this, coupled with raids by the French, led to the town's decline. Today the little 17th-century Town Hall is in the care of the National Trust, and the harbour is now a nature reserve, echoing to the piping of the curlew and the harsh cry of wild geese.

At the head of one of the creeks is Shalfleet, where you can explore the old harbour on foot, heading down to the quay which is now busy with pleasure craft. Shalfleet's Church of St Michael was saved in a small-scale replay of the saving of Winchester Cathedral. When its stout Norman tower was found to be standing in 10 feet (3m) of clay and water and in danger of collapsing, the foundations were relaid in concrete.

OSBORNE HOUSE

MAP REF SZ5296

Osborne House, overlooking the Solent to the east of Cowes, was designed as a royal country retreat by Prince Albert and Thomas Cubitt in the fashionable style of a Neapolitan villa, complete with stylish Italianate campaniles and a loggia. Started in 1845, it served both as a family home and for state functions, and this duality is reflected in the mix of homely and grand interiors on display today. Private rooms include the sitting room where the Queen and her consort worked together. Grander state rooms include the Durbar Room, which has an Indian-style plasterwork ceiling, where a selection of Indian gifts presented to Victoria, Empress of India, are displayed.

Outside are terraced gardens and a walled fruit and flower garden. In the grounds is the lovely Swiss Cottage, a child-size royal playhouse, charmingly furnished in miniature. The playhouse had a serious purpose, too: the royal princes learned about carpentry here, the princesses learned how to cook and manage a household, and each child had a garden plot in which to grow some vegetables and flowers. A museum next door shows mementoes collected by the Queen's children and grandchildren.

Victoria and Albert loved to walk in the woods at Osborne, and the Prince added to these extensively, planting every sort of British tree. The Queen recorded lovingly in her memoirs that nightingales were frequently to be heard.

Queen Victoria died at Osborne House, in 1901, and her successor Edward VII presented the well-loved mansion to the nation.

Nearby Barton is a much older place, with a medieval manor house rebuilt by Prince Albert as an experimental farm. Today its gardens are open to the public, along with an award-winning vineyard.

■ Insight

OSBORNE HOUSE

During the First World War, Osborne House became a convalescent home for officers. Among the men who came here were A A Milne, (creator of Winnie the Pooh), and Robert Graves, who recalled his stay in *Goodbye to All That* (1929).

A linear ride from Cowes to Newport

This ride makes a relaxed day out, with easy access from the mainland. There is a lot to see from the safe, level trail, which follows the National Cycle Network route along the former Cowes-to-Newport railway line. Route-finding is straightforward, and you'll enjoy some lovely views across the River Medina, with plenty of opportunities for birding on the way.

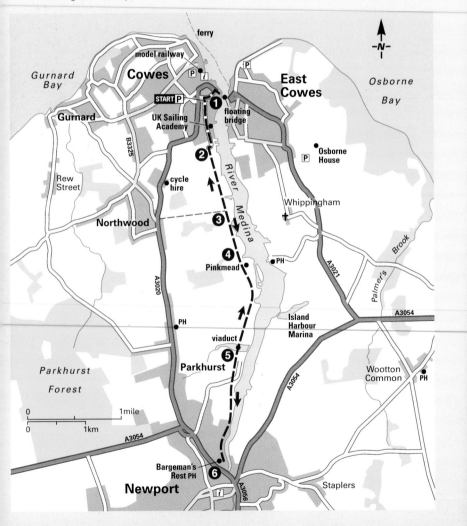

Route Directions

1 From Medina Road turn into Bridge Road, signposted 'Newport via cycleway'. Follow the road to the mini-roundabout at the top of the hill and turn left into Arctic Road, still following the signposted cycle route. Pass the UK Sailing Academy on your left and continue to the very end of the road.

2 Zig-zag right and left as the cycle route joins the old railway line, which edges its way clear of industrial Cowes through a tunnel of trees. Pass the signposted footpath to Northwood on your right and, a little further on, look out for the broken remains of an old iron and timber bridge.

3 Beyond the bridge, look out for a distinctive tall spire and pinnacles above the trees across the river. Around half a mile (800m) from the gates of Osborne House, St Mildred's church at Whippingham was remodelled in the mid-18th century for use by the royal family. Continue straight on along the track.

4 Now the views start to really open up, and between Pinkmead and Stag Lane you'll spot the old Ryde paddle steamer slowly rusting in her mud berth at Island Harbour Marina on the opposite bank. The hedges are thick with blackthorn, dog rose and crab apple, and in summer you'll see red admiral butterflies and dragonflies. Listen, too, for the plaintive call of curlews.

5 Now the trail crosses the old trestle viaduct that once carried the railway line over Dodnor Creek. This area of open water, marshland and woodland was created in the 1790s when the creek was dammed to provide power for a proposed tide mill. Today the creek is a local nature reserve and you may see reed warblers, coots, moorhens and grey herons. Beyond the creek the cycleway climbs briefly across Dodnor Lane and approaches industrial buildings on the edge of Newport. Look out for a pair of concrete tracks that cross the trail and lead to a pair of slim concrete jetties built out into the river. A rolling gantry loads industrial products onto waiting barges. The facility was specially designed to minimise disturbance to the birds feeding on the mudflats of this protected wildlife site. Soon, reach the white gate at the end of the traffic-free route. Continue straight ahead as far as the post-box on the corner of Hurstake Road. Turn left to The Bargeman's Rest, and bear right at the bottom of the hill for the final 300yds (274m) to the pub.

6 Take a break before retracing your route to Cowes.

Route facts

DISTANCE/TIME 8 miles (12.9km) 1h45

MAP OS Explorer OL29 Isle of Wight

START Medina Road pay-and-display car park, West Cowes, grid ref: SZ 499956

TRACKS Back streets of Cowes, tarred and level cycle track

GETTING TO THE START Take the A3020 from Newport to West Cowes and follow signs to the floating bridge. Passengers arriving with their bikes on the car ferry should follow the one-way system to the right, and cross the floating bridge to begin the ride in Medina Road, West Cowes.

CYCLE HIRE Top Gear Cycle Hire, 1 Terminus Road, Cowes. Tel: 01983 299056

THE PUB The Bargeman's Rest, Newport. Tel: 01983 525828; www.bargemansrest.com

❶ A short hill to begin and two sections of road. Ideal for beginners and children aged eight and over.

RYDE MAP REF SZ5993

When island visitors disembark at Ryde from the Portsmouth ferry, ex-London Transport underground trains take them down the 0.5-mile (800m) long pier, necessary because the coast shelves so gently that vessels can get no closer.

Ryde was developed in the late 18th century and is the largest town on the island, with some 24,000 residents. It has the usual seaside amusements as well as 5-mile (8km) long sandy beach. From the promenade there are superb views across Spithead and three of the Solent's Victorian forts. Ryde's summer carnival is a spectacular event.

Southwest of Ryde is Brickfields Horse Country, with horses of all sizes, wagon rides and pig-racing. At Ashey, Rosemary Vineyard, the largest of the island's three vineyards, offers tours, tastings and a shop. At Fishbourne, to the west, is Quarr Abbey, a modern foundation (1907–14) of Benedictine monks near the ruins of the earlier Cistercian Abbey. The Isle of Wight Steam Railway puffs out of Smallbrook Junction, just south of Ryde on its journey past Havenstreet to Wootton.

SANDOWN & SHANKLIN
MAP REF SZ5984

The honky-tonk seaside neighbour of more sedate Shanklin, Sandown was founded as a resort in about 1800 and faces southeastwards out to sea across Sandown Bay. It is built at beach level, with the immense chalk walls of Culver Cliff to the north and the cliffed coast of Shanklin and Luccombe to the south. Sandown is a popular venue for family holidays, with its 6 miles (9.7km) of sandy beach and an esplanade and amusement park, a pier of 1878, cinema, zoo specialising in tigers and lemurs, and the fascinating Dinosaur Isle, a museum displaying life-size dinosaurs and offering guided fossil walks. At the Garlic Farm, near Newchurch, you can buy and learn more.

Shanklin, the quieter neighbour to the south, is a resort that developed with the coming of the railway in 1891, and now has the best collection of beach huts on the island. You reach the beach by a lift from the clifftop, which has a superb view around Sandown Bay to the gleaming white heights of Culver Cliff. Inland is Shanklin Old Village, a former fishing village close to the winding glen of Shanklin Chine. This 300-feet (91.5m) deep, wooded and ferny fissure was much beloved of earlier tourists, including the poet, John Keats, who stayed at the Old Village in 1819 and composed part of *Endymion* here. The Victorians flocked to tread its winding path past the 40-foot (12m) waterfall to the beach. Today, Shanklin Chine still pulls the crowds – its rare flora is of great interest – and the resort also has two theatres and seaside amusements.

SEAVIEW MAP REF SZ6392

This family holiday resort to the east of Ryde is renowned for its gently sloping, firm, sandy beach, from which there is safe bathing. The town still basks in 19th-century charm, with narrow streets lined with villas and shops sloping down to the sea, the peace maintained by the lack of a main through road. Saltern

Cottages are a reminder of the old salt industry which thrived here on the bleak marshes in the days before Seaview became a select resort for those who shun the bustle and gaiety of Ryde. To the northwest is the famous Seaview Wildlife Encounter (formerly Flamingo Park), a bird sanctuary where flamingos, peacocks and waterfowl wander freely over green lawns.

VENTNOR MAP REF SZ5777

This south coast resort climbs the sheer cliff beneath flat St Boniface Down (the highest point on the island), as a series of terraces behind the sandy beach, so that the mainly Victorian buildings are built-up in layers and are joined by steep zig-zagging roads with corkscrew turns. There is something Mediterranean in this arrangement, and Ventnor has been dubbed 'the English Madeira'. Also, the climate, too, is very good. Protected by the bulk of St Boniface Down, it basks in subtropical conditions.

Ventnor was a small fishing village up until 1841 – albeit much involved in smuggling – but in that year, a famous doctor, Sir James Clarke, publicly sang its praises and visitors started to come. The railway arrived in 1866, meaning Ventnor's development as a health resort was assured, attracting, among others, authors Macaulay, Dickens and Thackeray. Later it was the site of the Royal National Hospital for Consumption and Diseases of the Chest. The town's history is explained in Ventnor's Heritage Museum which has an extensive archive.

Ventnor divides into two parts, the elegant 'town' on the cliff face, where

■ Visit

THE AUSTRALIAN CONNECTION

In the days when convicts were transported to Australia, most of them left Britain from ships moored off Ryde – the last they ever saw of 'the old country'. Because of this there remains a special connection between the town and Australia. St Thomas' Church is now a heritage centre with an exhibition commemorating the first ships that carried prisoners to Australia, as well as displays of other local history.

■ Insight

THE LOSS OF THE *EURIDICE*

In 1878 a fine, fully rigged sailing frigate sank off Dunnose Head, south of Shanklin, with the loss of 300 souls. The *Euridice* was a Royal Navy training ship, on her way to Bermuda with a full complement of passengers and crew. It was March and the weather was terrible, but sheltered in the lee of the cliffs, the ship sailed on in ignorance of the true conditions, its portholes open to ventilate the two decks. As she rounded the point and the true storm hit, she took on water and sank in the freezing waters.

■ Insight

OLD MONEY

According to local history, Yarmouth man and hero Robert Holmes (1622–1692) sailed with the King's fleet to Guinea, which is off the west coast of Africa. During this service Holmes' ship took aggressive action against a vessel that belonged to the Dutch West India Company which resulted in a large amount of Dutch gold allegedly being shipped back to England by Holmes. This gold was then melted down and made into coins – known as 'guineas'.

YARMOUTH

Ventnor ales are still brewed, and the seaside resort at the foot of the cliff. The extraordinary climate is manifest in the Ventnor Botanic Gardens, planted in the 1970s, where some 3,500 species include palms and cork trees. The interesting Smuggling Museum, hidden in subterranean caverns beneath the Botanic Garden, has a large collection of fascinating relics, vividly illustrating the days when Ventnor was the unofficial 'headquarters' of illicit trade. Near by is the ancient village of St Lawrence with the Rare Breeds and Waterfowl Park. Isle of Wight Glass, founded in 1973, produces an exciting range of award-winning glassware.

The southern coast between Ventnor and St Catherine's Point is a region of landslides, where great masses of sandstone rock have been, and continue to be, carried down into the sea on a lubricating layer of blue clay. In fact, Ventnor has the biggest urban landslide problem in Britain. The Undercliff, a ledge which extends along the cliffs, is actually the top of an ancient landslide block. To appreciate the coast to the full, walk part of the coastal path between Shanklin and Blackgang. From Shanklin the path first lies close to, and then on, the shore until Ventnor and beyond. At St Lawrence, the path climbs up beyond the road and affords good views to the south before you reach Blackgang.

Nearby Blackgang Chine is an extraordinary theme park that combines static displays with fast fairground rides and lovely gardens. In fact the gardens were the initial inspiration for the park, created to attract Victorian vacationers.

YARMOUTH MAP REF SZ3689

The Lymington–Yarmouth ferry is the picturesque way of entry to the Isle of Wight, for Yarmouth is a compact little town with narrow streets and attractive houses, and a small harbour busy with yachts and a flourishing boatbuilder's yard. During the Middle Ages it was the most important Isle of Wight town, but decline set in and by 1800 it had only a few hundred inhabitants.

Yarmouth's sturdy castle was built against the French in 1547 by Henry VIII, and it remained in use until the 1870s. It is hidden down an alley by the ferry, on King's Land, and is easy to miss. The pier near the lifeboat station was built in 1876 and was originally the landing stage for the Lymington ferry, but now it is a pleasant walkway.

Yarmouth's church, rebuilt 1614–26, contains an intriguing monument to Sir Robert Holmes, Governor of the Isle of Wight during the reign of Charles II. The figure was originally intended as a statue of the French 'Sun King', Louis XIV. The statue was being transported by sea so that the sculptor could complete the head from life, but Holmes captured the ship carrying it, took the statue and had his own likeness attached to it instead. Holmes entertained Charles II at his house on the quay in Yarmouth, now the George Hotel.

West of Yarmouth is Fort Victoria Country Park, based around the remains of a fort built in 1855. The many parts of the park afford superb views of the Solent, and there are guided walks, an interesting maritime heritage exhibition, a marine aquarium and planetarium.

Around Freshwater

West Wight is a peaceful area of great natural beauty, offering swathes of open countryside, cliffs, wonderful views and fascinating wildlife. This ramble encapsulates the contrasting landscapes of the area, from rolling farmland and the magnificent chalk headlands and hills with their breathtaking coastal views. If you have time, you could divert to explore the wildlife-rich tidal estuary of the River Yar and the freshwater marshes that are home to many species of wild birds.

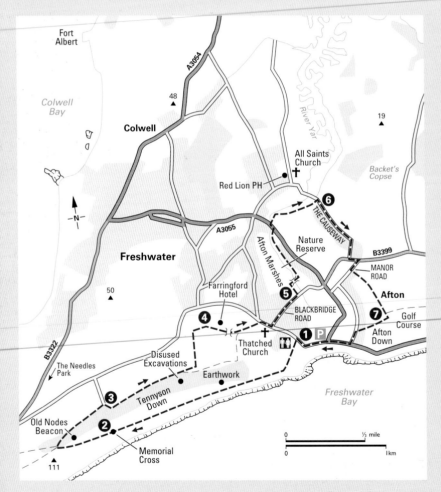

Route Directions

1 From the car park, turn right along the road, then left before the bus shelter along a metalled track, signed 'Coastal Path'. After 50yds (46m) bear right through a gate and follow the well-walked path through a gateway and up to the memorial cross at the summit of Tennyson Down.

2 Continue down the wide grassy swathe, which narrows between gorse bushes, to reach the replica of the Old Nodes Beacon. Here, turn very sharp right down a chalk track. At a junction (car park right) keep straight on up the narrow path.

3 The path widens, then descends to a gate into woodland. Proceed close to the woodland fringe before emerging into more open countryside. Just beyond a disused pit on your right, fork left at a waymark post down a narrower path. Cross a stile, then follow the enclosed path as it turns sharp left to a stile. Cross the next field to a stile and turn right along the field-edge to a stile.

4 Cross a farm track, go through a gate and walk along the track (F47) beside Farringford Hotel. Pass beneath a wooden footbridge and continue downhill to a gate and the road. (Turn left if you wish to visit the hotel.) Turn right; then, opposite the thatched church, turn left down Blackbridge Road. Just before Black Bridge, turn left into Afton Marshes Nature Reserve.

5 Join the nature trail, following it across a footbridge and beside the stream to the A3055 (this can be very wet in winter). Turn left and almost immediately cross over to join bridleway (F61) along the course of the old railway. In 0.5 mile (800m) reach the Causeway. Turn left here to visit Freshwater church and the Red Lion.

6 To continue on the route turn right and continue to the B3399. Turn left and shortly cross on to unmetalled Manor Road. In a few paces, bear left, signed 'Freshwater Way', and ascend across grassland towards Afton Down.

7 Keep ahead at a junction of paths beside the golf course, soon to follow the gravel track right to the clubhouse. Go through a gate, pass in front of the building to reach the access track, keeping left to the A3055. Turn right downhill into Freshwater Bay.

Route facts

DISTANCE/TIME
5.75 miles (9.2km) 3h

MAP OS Explorer OL29
Isle of Wight

START Pay-and-display car park, Freshwater Bay, grid ref: SZ 346857

TRACKS Downland, field and woodland paths, some road walking and stretch of disused railway, 4 stiles

GETTING TO THE START
Freshwater is in the west of the Isle of Wight, inland from Yarmouth.

THE PUB The Red Lion, Church Place, Freshwater. Tel: 01983 754925

■ TOURIST INFORMATION CENTRES

Cowes
The Arcade, Fountain Quay.
Tel: 01983 813818

Newport
The Guildhall, High Street.
Tel: 01983 813818

Ryde
Western Esplanade.
Tel: 01983 813818

Sandown
8 High Street.
Tel: 01983 813818

Shanklin
67 High Street.
Tel: 01983 813818

Yarmouth
The Quay.
Tel: 01983 813818

■ PLACES OF INTEREST

Adgestone Vineyard
Brading.
Tel: 01983 402503;
www.adgestonevineyard.co.uk

Appuldurcombe House
Godshill.
Tel: 01983 852484;
www.appuldurcombe.co.uk

Barton Manor Gardens & Vineyard
East Cowes.
Tel: 01983 280676

Bembridge Windmill (NT)
High Street, Bembridge.
Tel: 01983 873945;

Brading Roman Villa
Brading.
Tel: 01983 406223;
www.bradingromanvilla.org.uk

Calbourne Water Mill
Tel: 01983 531227;
www.calbournewatermill.co.uk

Carisbrooke Castle & Isle of Wight Museum (EH)
1.5 miles (2.4km) southeast of Newport.
Tel: 01983 522107

Fort Victoria Country Park
Near Yarmouth.
Tel: 01983 823893;
www.fortvictoria.co.uk

Heritage Museum
11 Spring Hill, Ventnor.
Tel: 01983 855407;
www.ventnorheritage.org.uk

Isle of Wight Steam Railway
Tel: 01983 884343;
www.iwsteamrailway.co.uk

The Lilliput Antique Doll & Toy Museum
Brading. Tel: 01983 407231

Maritime Museum
Beckford Road, Cowes.
Tel: 01983 823433

Mottistone Manor Garden (NT)
Tel: 01983 741302

Museum of Island History
Guildhall, Newport.
Tel: 01983 823366;
www.iwight.com

The Needles Old Battery (NT)
West Highdown, Totland.
Tel: 0871 720 0022

The Needles Park
Tel: 0870 458 0022;
www.theneedles.co.uk

Newport Roman Villa
Cypress Road, Newport.
Tel: 01983 529720;
www.romans-in-britain.org.uk

Nostalgia Toy Museum
High Street, Godshill.
Tel: 01983 840181

Osborne House & Gardens (EH)
East Cowes.
Tel: 01983 200022

Rosemary Vineyard
Ashey, Ryde.
Tel: 01983 811084;
www.rosemaryvineyard.co.uk

Shanklin Chine
Shanklin.
Tel: 01983 866432;
www.shanklinchine.co.uk

Smuggling Museum
Botanic Garden, Ventnor.
Tel: 01983 853677

Yarmouth Castle (EH)
Yarmouth.
Tel: 01983 760678

■ FOR CHILDREN

Amazon World Zoo Park
Watery Lane, near Arreton.
Tel: 01983 867122;
www.amazonworld.co.uk

Blackgang Chine
Chale, near Ventnor.
Tel: 01983 730052;
www.blackgangchine.com

Godshill Model Village
Old Vicarage Gardens, Godshill.
Tel: 01983 840270; www.modelvillagegodshill.co.uk

Isle of Wight Owl and Falconry Centre
Appledurcombe.
Tel: 01983 852484;
www.appledurcombe.co.uk

Isle of Wight Zoo
Yaverland Seafront, Sandown.
Tel: 01983 403883;
www.isleofwightzoo.com

Seaview Wildlife Encounter
Tel: 01983 612261;
www.flamingoparkiw.com

■ SHOPPING

Arreton Barns Craft Village
Main Road, Arreton.
Tel: 01983 539361;
www.arretonbarns.co.uk

Bonchurch Pottery
Shore Road, Bonchurch.
Tel: 01983 854445

The Cider Barn
High Street, Godshill.
Tel: 01983 840680

Isle of Wight Farmers' Market
St Thomas' Square, Newport.
Every Fri.

■ PERFORMING ARTS

Medina Theatre
Fairlee Road, Newport.
Tel: 01983 527020

Ryde Theatre
Lind Street, Ryde.
Tel: 01983 568099

Shanklin Theatre
Prospect Road, Shanklin.
Tel: 01983 862739

■ SPORTS & ACTIVITIES

ADRENALINE SPORTS

Wight Water Adventure Watersports
Tel: 01983 404987;
www.wightwaters.com

First Contact
Tel: 01983 6741484
Paragliding and fast boats.

BOAT TRIPS

Needles Pleasure Cruises
Tel: 01983 761587

CYCLE HIRE

Battersby Cycles
Ryde.
Tel: 01983 562039

Church Street Cycles
Ventnor.
Tel: 01983 852232

Wight Cycle Hire
Tel: 01983 761800;
www.wightcyclehire.co.uk

FISHING

Island Fish Farm & Meadow Lakes
Muggleton Lane,
near Brighstone.
Tel: 01983 740941

Scotties Fishing Tackle
11 Lugley Street,
Newport.
Tel: 01983 522115;
www.scotties-tackle.co.uk

HORSE-RIDING

Allendale Equestrian Centre
Newport Road,
Godshill.
Tel: 01983 840258

Brickfields Horse Country
Binstead, near Ryde.
Tel: 01983 566801;
www.brickfields.net

■ ANNUAL EVENTS & CUSTOMS

Cowes
Cowes Week;
late Jul–early Aug.
Tel: 01983 295744;
www.cowesweek.co.uk

Isle of Wight County Show
Northwood Showground,
mid-Aug. Tel: 01983 826275;
www.riwas.org.uk

Newchurch
Garlic Festival, mid-Aug.
Tel: 01983 614612;
www.garlic-festival.co.uk

Newport
Isle of Wight Festival; pop
festival; mid-Jun.
Tel: 08444 999955;
www.isleofwightfestival.org

Ryde
Carnival, end Aug/early Sep.

Yarmouth
Old Gaffers Festival,
gaff-rigged yachts; early Jun.
Tel: 01983 761704;
www.yarmoutholdgaffers
festival.co.uk

Isle of Wight Cycling Festival
Mid-Sep.
Tel: 01983 823355;
www.sunseaandcycling.com

Isle of Wight Walking Festival
Mid-May.
Tel: 01983 823070;
www.isleofwightwalking
festival.co.uk.

Round the Island Race
Mid-Jun.
Tel: 01983 296621;
www.roundtheisland.org.uk

Tea Rooms

Vineyard Café

Adgestone Vineyard,
Upper Adgestone Road,
Brading PO36 0ES
Tel: 01983 402503;
www.adgestonevineyard.co.uk
The oldest vineyard in Britain
serves some of the best
cream teas on the Isle of
Wight, with freshly baked
scones, and home-made
cakes. Morning coffee and
light lunches – including
wine – are also available,
and check ahead for special
musical evenings.

God's Providence House

12 St Thomas Square,
Newport PL30 1SL
Tel: 01983 522085
This is the spot where, it is
claimed, the Great Plague of
the 1560s came to a halt –
hence the name. Today it's a
traditional tea room, serving
coffee, teas and lunches.

Chessell Pottery Café

Brook Road,
Yarmouth PO41 0UE
Tel: 01983 531248;
www.pottery-café.com
The pretty courtyard is a
lovely setting for making your
own pottery or enjoying an
'Ultimate Island Cream Tea'.
The clotted cream is from a
local farm and the strawberry
jam is also made near by.

The Old World Tearooms & Gardens

The High Street,
Godshill PO38 3HZ
Tel: 01983 840637
This popular, family-run tea
room in the lovely village of
Godshill serves delicious
cream teas, morning coffee,
light lunches, and a good
range of sandwiches and
baguettes. Eat indoors or out.

Pubs

Buddle Inn

St Catherines Road,
Niton PO38 2NE
Tel: 01983 730243;
www.buddleinn.co.uk
This is one of the island's
oldest hostelries in a former
16th-century farmhouse.
There are stone flags, oak
beams and a large open fire.
Dogs and muddy boots are
welcome. Home-cooked food
includes crab and lobster,
curries and ploughman's,
and there's a good choice
of wines and real ales.

The Folly

Folly Lane, Cowes PO32 6LY
Tel: 01983 297171
Easy access by both land and
water makes this unusual
Cowes pub a very popular
venue in summer. It was
constructed in part from the
timbers out of the hull of an
old barge, and makes good
use of its nautical theme,
offering a blackboard menu
that includes spicy sausage
'Crewpot' casserole, or
maybe fresh fish.

The New Inn

Mill Lane,
Shalfleet PO30 4NE
Tel: 01983 531314;
www.thenew-inn.co.uk
Beamed ceilings, a flagstone
floor and big open fireplaces
characterise this fine 18th-
century inn on the coastal
path route. They specialise
in fish and seafood, with
offerings such as hake with
tarragon and lemon.
Specials include more
seafood and fish as well
as meat dishes. There are
around 60 wines, plus beers
such as Flowers Bitter and
Marston's Pedigree.

The Red Lion

Church Place,
Freshwater PO40 9PB
Tel: 01983 754925
The pub has a pleasant
setting on the River Yar, and
everything here is freshly
made. Favourites might
include gammon with parsley
sauce, smoked haddock pâté,
and apple pie and custard.
The garden includes a herb
garden – the perfect place to
sup a pint of local Goddards
ale – and dogs are permitted.

Portsmouth & Southeast Coast

The great Hampshire ports, commercial Southampton and naval fleet-based Portsmouth, comprise the largest urban area on England's south coast. During the 20th century they spread, eating up lesser harbours and towns and creeping inland. Among all this are the nature reserves at Langstone Harbour and Titchfield Haven, the popular beaches around Southsea, and the many marinas that line the Solent's shores. Wartime memories abound in this area, too – thousands of men, women and boats congregated here for the invasion of occupied Europe during the Second World War.

7 Walk start point

HMS WARRIOR, PORTSMOUTH

BATTLESHIPS, PORTSMOUTH HARBOUR

Unmissable attractions

Go to the top of Portsmouth's striking Spinnaker Tower for superb views over the British Navy's most important historical base...see the coastal differences by walking part of the Solent Way...spend, spend, spend at Southampton's glossy West Quay shopping centre...witness boat-building at its best on The Hamble...marvel at 3rd-century Roman Portchester Castle...come face to face with a shark at Southsea's fantastic Blue Reef Aquarium...visit writer William Cobbett's beloved Botley.

1

1 Spinnaker Tower

Most people choose to use the lift, rather than climb the 572 steps to viewing deck three. Apart from the awesome panorama, there is a challenging view down through a glass floor. Do you dare to step onto it?

2 HMS *Victory*

The prow of Admiral Horatio Nelson's flagship HMS *Victory*, has been beautifully restored and can be admired at Portsmouth Maritime Museum.

3 Netley Abbey

The abbey is one of the best preserved medieval Cistercian monasteries in the south of England.

BOTLEY MAP REF SU5213

The political writer and champion of the underdog William Cobbett farmed here between 1804 and 1817. He described this attractive redbrick village, where he was actually constantly quarrelling with the local parson, as 'the most delightful village in the world', and he is fondly celebrated with a memorable stone in the village square and a walking trail around the village. Botley was once a small port at the head of the Hamble River. The village remains delightful, its wide main street and busy square dominated by a little porticoed Market Hall of 1848. The mill on the River Hamble, listed in the Domesday Book, is now a crafts centre.

Just to the south, extensive Manor Farm Country Park, 400 acres (162ha) of varied habitats, supports a range of plants and animals, with riverside and woodland walks. The park's Manor Farm Museum is a traditional farm offering hands-on experience of pigs, cows and other livestock. East of Botley, Wickham Vineyard offers a taste of English wines.

■ Insight

WILLIAM COBBETT

Born in Fareham in 1763, William Cobbett was a self-educated man with forthright views. After fleeing to America to avoid prosecution, he developed his talents as a pamphleteer. He returned to England in 1802 to start a newspaper, travelled and wrote books, including *Rural Rides* (1830), an account of his travels across southern England. He supported the underdog in a pithy and opinionated style, adopting more radical anti-government views. In 1832 he became a Member of Parliament.

FAREHAM MAP REF SU5706

Fareham's attractive old High Street has a complementary mix of architecture – 18th-century brick, Victorian stucco and earlier timber. Since the Second World War the old town has expanded and now merges with neighbouring parishes in a sprawl of houses and industry. The centre still remains appealing, and visitors can appreciate the 19th-century novelist William Thackeray's description of it as a 'dear little old Hampshire town'.

During the Middle Ages Fareham was a major port, until the channels silted up. Prosperity returned in the 18th and 19th centuries with shipbuilding for the navy, and the big, attractive houses on the High Street were built for senior naval men. Today there are high-tech industries as well as an entertainment centre and a shopping mall. Fareham Creek, popular with the yachting fraternity, is now a conservation area.

In 1784 at Funtley, near Fareham, Henry Cort invented a process of creating wrought iron which helped keep Britain's economy together during the Napoleonic Wars. British iron ores are generally low grade, and during the wars, foreign ores could not get through – a potentially disastrous state of affairs affecting the production of horseshoes, tools and nails. Cort devised the method of 'puddling', where the molten metal was stirred with iron bars – a process that separated the ore from impurities and allowed the production of wrought iron. Little remains today of the iron works, but what there is can be seen beside the footpath off the Wickham to Titchfield road beside the M27.

HAMBLE MAP REF SU4807

Once a main site of a flourishing naval dockyard, the village of Hamble and the estuary of the little river that shares its name are still popular with sailors of the small pleasure craft that crowd its busy waters as they sail or motor in and out of Southampton Water. The older parts of the village, unpretentious in brick, go down to the quayside near the jetties, the marina and the boat-building yards.

Hamble was a favoured place of embarkation during the Napoleonic Wars and troops were mustered here. In more recent times Hamble has had strong links with the aircraft industry, with a British Aerospace factory and airfield where airline pilots were trained.

The nearby village of Bursledon has the last steam-driven brickworks in the country, founded in 1897, and Hampshire's only working windmill.

HAYLING ISLAND

MAP REF SU7303

This small, popular island separates the tidal creeks, sprawling mudflats and low-lying saltmarshes of Langstone and Chichester harbours. The northern part is chiefly rural while the southern part, facing over the Channel, has been a resort since the mid-19th century. It has a 5-mile (8km) long sandy beach, select golf club and all the paraphernalia of a holiday resort devoted to water sports, particularly windsurfing. Drivers should note that there is only one road to and from the island, and it can get very busy. The seafront is dominated by the huge Norfolk Crescent, erected in the early 19th century. The 13th-century church at

■ Insight

SAILING ON THE SOLENT

The Solent is said to contain the largest pleasure sailing fleet in the world, with more than 32,000 yacht berths in the plethora of marinas along the coast stretching from Southampton Water to Chichester Harbour. The sailing is safe here, in the sheltered lagoons of Portsmouth, Langstone and Chichester harbours, in Southampton Water and in the Solent, where craft are protected from the open Channel by the Isle of Wight. Hamble is the yachting capital of Southampton Water and Ocean Village, in Southampton's old Alexandra Dock, is a superb marina where hundreds of yachts are moored, and where there are shops and restaurants.

South Hayling stands on the island's highest point – the yew tree in the churchyard is a true Saxon, probably 1,000 years old; the Saxon font is one of only a handful of that age in Hampshire.

Sandy Point to the southeast and Langstone Harbour along to the west are designated nature reserves and both are important overwintering grounds for geese and waders. Langstone Harbour is the central of three shallow lagoons and remains a mostly wild, saltmarsh-girt, muddy place. The harbour itself covers some 5,000 acres (2,025ha) and contains a 1,370-acre (555ha) RSPB reserve, at its best in September and through the winter when it is full of migrant waders, including Brent geese, dunlin, turnstones and rare black-tailed godwits. There are frequent sightings of resident oystercatchers, redshanks, herons and shelducks.

A circuit from Hamble to Bursledon

The villages of Hamble and Old Bursledon are a delight to explore. Hamble has a twisting main street, lined with pretty Georgian buildings, leading down to the Quay with lovely river views. Old Bursledon has peaceful lanes dotted with interesting buildings. Tucked away on the slopes above the river, you'll find it a pleasure to stroll through lanes going nowhere, especially if you stop at the Hacketts Marsh viewpoint.

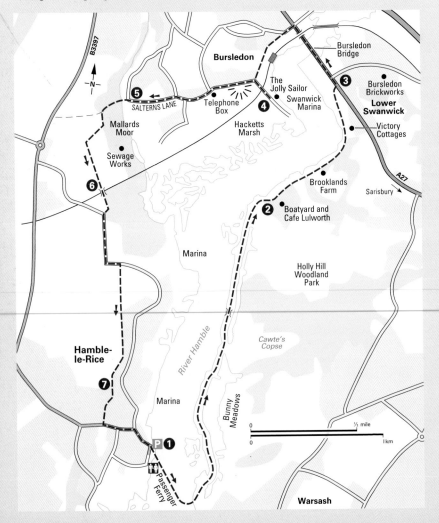

Route Directions

1 From the quayside car park, walk to the pontoon and take the passenger ferry across the estuary to Warsash (weather permitting; for details, visit www.hamble-warsashferry.co.uk). Turn left along the raised gravel path beside the estuary and mudflats. Cross a footbridge and continue to a gravelled parking area. During exceptionally high tides the path may flood, so walk through the car park and rejoin it by the marina.

2 Follow the path through a boatyard, pass in front of Cafe Lulworth, and rejoin the riverside path. Keep ahead at a lane, pass Victory Cottages on your right, and continue to the A27.

3 Turn left, pass Swanwick Marina, and cross Bursledon Bridge. (Turn right before the bridge to visit Bursledon Brickworks.) Pass under the railway, turn left into Church Lane, then fork left. Turn left into Station Road. Turn left into the station car park, following signs for the Jolly Sailor. Climb a steep path to the road. Turn left at the junction, then left again to the pub.

4 Return along the lane and fork left along the High Street into Old Bursledon. Pause at the viewpoint at Hacketts Marsh, then bear left at the telephone box along the High Street. Pass the Vine Inn and Salterns Lane, then at a right bend, bear off left by Thatched Cottage along a footpath.

5 Join a metalled lane beside the drive to the Coach House then, as the lane curves right, keep ahead beside a house called Woodlands, following the bridleway downhill to a stream. Proceed uphill through woodland (Mallards Moor). At a junction of paths on the woodland fringe, bear left with the bridleway, then at a concrete road bear right, then left to join a fenced bridleway.

6 Cross a railway bridge and soon pass a barrier to a road. Keep left round a sharp left-hand bend. Look out for a waymarked footpath on your right and follow this path behind houses for 0.5mile (800m).

7 Join a metalled path and keep ahead past modern housing to a road. Follow this out to Hamble Lane and turn left to join the High Street. At the roundabout, bear right down Lower High Street back to the Quay and car park.

Route facts

DISTANCE/TIME
5.5 miles (8.8km) 3h

MAP OS Explorer OL22 New Forest

START Pay-and-display car park by the Quay, Hamble, grid ref: SU 485067

TRACKS Riverside, field and woodland paths, some stretches of road.

GETTING TO THE START The large village of Hamble is east of Southampton at the end of the B3397, 4 miles (6.4km) south of the M27, junction 8. At a mini-roundabout in the centre of Hamble take the narrow lane downhill to the Quay and car park.

THE PUB The Jolly Sailor, Lands End Road, Old Bursledon. Tel: 023 8040 5557

❶ Great care required along the estuary, especially at high tide, and along the roads at Hamble and Bursledon.

NETLEY MAP REF SU4608

Netley, a Victorian town on the shores of the Solent, was formerly important for three things – its castle, its abbey and its gigantic military hospital, the Royal Victoria, built in the aftermath of the Crimean War. This was demolished in 1966, bar the domed royal chapel, and the site is now occupied by the Royal Victoria Country Park which covers more than 100 acres (40ha) of mixed woods, marshes and beach. There is a nature trail, miniature railway and walks.

The ruins of Netley Abbey stand brooding in woodland next to the Solent shore. It was founded here in 1239 as a daughter house of Beaulieu and, as little is known of day to day life here, we must assume a most peaceful and prayerful existence on the part of the monks, until the Dissolution of the Monasteries. Netley Castle, on the shore near the abbey and formerly the gatehouse, was one of Henry VIII's coastal gun stations – its tall tower is Victorian, and it has been transformed into a wonderful folly with all the panoply of Gothic device (now luxury apartments).

PORTCHESTER CASTLE

MAP REF SU6305

This is one of the most fascinating historical sites in Britain. The massive, 20-foot (6m) high walls of a 3rd-century Roman fort sit on a little promontory on the northern shore of Portsmouth Harbour, facing directly across it and out to sea. The thick walls, 10-feet (3m) deep, enclose a large area of 9 acres (3.6ha), and make it the most complete Roman fort in northern Europe.

After the Roman withdrawal from Britain, Portchester's defences were left much as they were until 1133, when a priory was founded here by Henry I. It soon shifted inland to Southwick, but Portchester's parish church is a survivor of the monastic foundation. In 1153 the Normans took over the abandoned fort and built a keep on the northwest corner, plus a wall and moat enclosing an inner bailey. The castle was further fortified at regular intervals throughout history, and in 1415 Henry V mustered his troops on the greensward of the outer bailey and led them all through the Water Gate to embark for France and the Battle of Agincourt. Later it was used as a royal country palace, and in 1535 Henry VIII and Anne Boleyn stayed here and were 'very merry'. During the Napoleonic Wars, around 4,000 French prisoners were held within the walls.

PORTSMOUTH MAP REF SZ6498

Portsmouth has been Britain's foremost naval base since the late 15th century, when it had the first ever dry dock. For a great view over the city, take the lift to the top of the elegant 558-foot (170m) high Spinnaker Tower.

The town's biggest attraction is the collection of historic ships that can be visited in the Naval Dockyard. HMS *Victory*, launched in 1765, was Nelson's flagship at the Battle of Trafalgar in 1805 and is probably the most famous British warship; she is the oldest commissioned warship in the world. The *Mary Rose*, pride of Henry VIII's fleet, was launched at Portsmouth in 1511, rebuilt to carry more guns in 1536 and sank off

Southsea in July 1545, sailing to meet the French in battle, and in full view of the King who was watching from Southsea Castle. The remains of her wreck were finally raised in 1982 and are currently housed in a specially designed and constructed building. 'Permanent conservation' is under way, and there is an exhibition of the artefacts found during salvage. HMS *Warrior*, the first 'ironclad', was launched at Blackwall in 1860, the largest, fastest and most formidable warship the world had ever seen. The Dockyard also houses the redeveloped Royal Naval Museum and 'Action Stations', a thrilling high-tech Royal Naval experience using film and interactive technology.

During the Second World War Portsmouth was bombed heavily, and it is unfortunate that much of the rebuilding has been particularly uninspired – one building (since demolished) was voted the ugliest in Britain by readers of a certain Sunday newspaper. This being so, hurry through to the historic dockyard and follow the Millennium Promenade (Renaissance Trail) on foot through the bustling Gunwharf Quays shopping complex to The Point. Here is the oldest and most picturesque quarter of Old Portsmouth, where surviving attractive old streets have been restored, and face out onto a little harbour. This area of intricate little roads and Georgian and Victorian houses was known as 'Spice Island', an invocation of the exotic cargoes that arrived here. Walk on the old defences or linger by the seawall in Bath Square to watch the world and the shipping go by.

The city has more than a dozen museums, including Charles Dickens' Birthplace in Old Commercial Road, but the City Museum and Art Gallery found in Museum Road is probably the best place to start. It features 'The Story of Portsmouth' and will point you in the direction of the other remaining historic buildings around the city, including the Landport Gate of 1760, the Square Tower of 1494 and the Royal Garrison Church, where Catherine of Braganza married Charles II in 1662.

There are several good reasons to visit Gosport, just across Portsmouth Harbour, including the view back to Old Portsmouth, and to see the magnificent interior of Holy Trinity Church, which contains the organ once played by Handel. The main attraction, though, is the Royal Navy Submarine Museum, with exhibits relating to underwater warfare and submarine development, and tours of HMS *Alliance*, a submarine completed at the end of the Second World War. Gosport's Millennium Promenade takes in Timespace, one of the world's largest vertical sundials, erected in 2005, and Explosion!, a hands-on museum of naval firepower.

■ Activity

HARBOUR TRIPS

Take a relaxing boat trip around the harbour – with an informative running commentary, they give a genuine flavour of seafaring Portsmouth: modern naval vessels, ferries and the general hustle and bustle of this most important of naval ports. If taking to the sea is not for you, catch the little ferry over to Gosport, for a view back to Old Portsmouth.

SOUTHAMPTON MAP REF SU4213

Modern Southampton has been made by its docks. Its famous double tides give prolonged high water, and although the main container docks are not accessible to the public, there's a grand view of the comings and goings of cruise ships and the pleasure craft from Town Quay and Western Esplanade. This is a sprawling, thriving, working city, with attractions that include some of the best shopping along the south coast, the fine City Art Gallery, a string of leafy green parks, and a little Maritime Museum set in a 15th-century warehouse near the shore, which tells of the great liners built here, and the last, fateful voyage of the RMS *Titanic*. The Solent Sky Aviation Museum, which offers hands-on experience of many of the exhibits (try your hand at a supersonic jet!), was founded in honour of R J Mitchell, designer of the Spitfire fighter plane which was constructed at Southampton's Supermarine Works. A flying boat in the collection is another reminder of the port's history.

Southampton was very badly hit by bombing during the Second World War, and much rebuilding was done in haste and very cheaply. As a result, it is an unattractive architectural mishmash, but there are still some historic gems.

The most interesting area lies south of the gleaming West Quay shopping centre, and it is worth parking there to explore on foot. The mall has many well-known high street shops, including John Lewis and Marks & Spencer, and leads out onto Above Bar Street, a pedestrianised shopping street set above a bulky gateway, one of several last surviving fragments of the medieval walled city. Stroll down here, passing the Dolphin Hotel – novelist Jane Austen celebrated her 18th birthday on the first-floor ballroom here in 1793. Next door is the bombed-out Church of the Holy Rood, now dedicated to the merchant seamen of the city, and including a memorial to the 500 local crew who died aboard HMS *Titanic* when she sank in 1912. Beyond nearby St Michael's, the oldest church in the city, dating to 1070, and the only one undamaged in the war, lie Bugle Street and French Street, with the Medieval Merchant's House of 1290 and the striking timbered Tudor House Museum and Garden. Another little interesting corner to explore is Oxford Street, behind Queen's Terrace, its mellow old houses now filled with trendy restaurants, and with an Edwardian pub, the London Hotel, at one corner.

On the shore, ferries leave for the Isle of Wight and Hythe, and Ocean Village is a modern marina from where you can take a cruise of the harbour.

SOUTHSEA MAP REF SZ6698

Beyond the tangle of Old Portsmouth's streets to the east, you emerge on to Southsea Common, faced by imposing terraces of 19th-century stucco. The grassy common overlooking the sea escaped development during the 19th century because it was used for military training, and for this we must be very grateful as it gives Southsea its own distinctive flavour. Southsea developed as a residential suburb of Portsmouth, but the seaside location transformed it into a holiday place from the 1860s.

Today there is a raucous funfair at Clarence Pier. The wide Clarence Esplanade, between the common and the sea, has the fabulous Blue Reef Aquarium, the big Naval War Memorial and the Southsea Castle Museum. Near by, the D-Day Museum contains the remarkable Overlord Embroidery, a fine tapestry depicting the Allied invasion of Normandy in June 1944, paying homage to the Bayeux Tapestry of 1066.

Further east the pier provides boat trips and amusements, while on East Parade is the Cumberland House Natural History Museum. The Royal Marines Museum is housed in Eastney Barracks, beyond which are the Port Solent and Eastney Marinas. The Solent Way passes along the Southsea front.

During the 1860s four sea forts were built offshore, part of the ring of forts to protect Portsmouth and Spithead from a feared attack by the French. The smallest is Spitbank Fort, which had provision for nine 38-ton guns and can be visited by ferry from Southsea pier.

TITCHFIELD MAP REF SU5405

Titchfield, on the lower reaches of the River Meon, is a lovely village of twisting roads with a charming High Street. The aerospace factories on its outskirts create a curious juxtaposition of ancient and modern. In medieval times Titchfield was a market centre and a prosperous port, with a large and thriving abbey, founded in 1232. At the Dissolution the abbey passed to Thomas Wriothesley, the 1st Earl of Southampton, who then converted part of it into a house, but it fell into disrepair in the 18th century and

■ Activity

THE SOLENT WAY

This 60-mile (96km) path runs from Milford on Sea via Southampton and Portsmouth to the wild saltings of Langstone Harbour and Emsworth. The stretch from Warsash (or Hamble) to Emsworth begins along an undeveloped stretch of Solent coast between the Hamble River and Titchfield Haven, at the mouth of the River Meon, where there is a nature reserve. Beyond Titchfield Haven it goes past the beach at Lee-on-the-Solent and the lovely curve of Stokes Bay, turning inland at Gilkicker Point for the ferry from Gosport to Old Portsmouth. From here it passes Southsea to the edge of Langstone Harbour, before curving to Emsworth.

is now in ruins, split off from the village by the A27. Little of the original abbey remains but a huge Tudor gatehouse. A 15th-century tithe barn stands near by.

The 1st Earl also instituted a land reclamation scheme, damming the mouth of the river and building a canal. One of England's earliest canals, it was too small for merchant ships and Titchfield's days as a port were soon over. The Earl has not been forgiven, and his effigy is burnt at celebrations in October organised by the Bonfire Boys.

A different – and magnificent – effigy of the Earl can be found in the south chapel of the church. The detailed Wriothesley Monument by artist Gerard Johnson, a Flemish refugee, was carved in 1594 and shows the 1st Earl with his wife and son. The 3rd Earl was a friend of William Shakespeare, and it is said that some of his plays received their first performance here.

A wander from Wickham

With its medieval market square and engaging collection of independent shops, Wickham, at the heart of the Forest of Bere, is one of Hampshire's most attractive little towns. It was the birthplace of William of Wykeham, founder of both Winchester College and New College, Oxford.

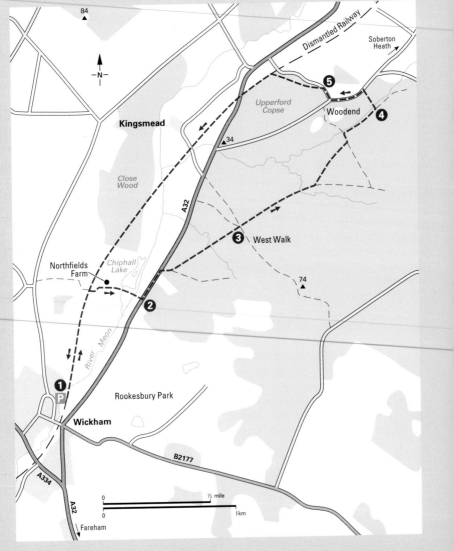

Route Directions

1 The Station car park on the north-east outskirts of Wickham backs directly on to the bridleway. Turn left, heading north and leaving the bridge over the River Meon behind you. Follow the old line as far as the first overbridge; 60yds (55m) beyond the brick arch, take the path that doubles back to the left and climb up to the farm track at the top. Turn left, cross over the railway and follow the track as it winds past the picturesque Northfields Farm and Chiphall Lake to the A32.

2 There is no footway here so cross over, turn left, and take great care as you follow the busy main road for 200yds (183m), passing two lodge cottages on the right-hand side. Then, just beyond Chiphall Paddock, turn right past a wooden barrier into West Walk. Follow the gravelled track at right angles to the road for the first 75yds (69m), then fork left on to a forest path. Ignore all turnings, and keep ahead as the trail dips into a small valley, crosses a brook, and climbs 300yds (274m) to a five-way junction.

3 Keep ahead here, signed towards West Walk and Woodend. Continue over the next crossways (signed 'West Walk') and, 220yds (201m) further on, fork left onto a narrower gravel track. Keep ahead at a crossways, then fork left, dropping down to cross a gravelled forest ride. Continue for 320yds (293m), and take a turning on the left.

4 Immediately cross a tiny brook, climb the short hill and, after 200yds (183m), leave the forest at a gate on the road to Soberton Heath. Turn left, then take the first turning on the right, signposted to Swanmore and Curdridge. Follow the road for 250yds (229m), as far as a small lay-by on the left-hand side.

5 Here you'll find the start of a rather unpromising little path, which improves as it drops down beside a post and rail fence towards the old railway track. Join the disused line just south of the road bridge and turn left and continue along here for 2 miles (3.2km), back to the start.

Route facts

DISTANCE/TIME
4.5 miles (7.2km) 2h

MAP OS Explorer 119 Meon Valley & Portsmouth

START Station Car Park, Wickham, grid ref: SU 574116

TRACKS Bridleways and forest tracks – will be muddy after rain; 2-mile (3.6km) stretch along dismantled railway

GETTING TO THE START
Wickham is 3 miles (4.8km) north of Fareham and can be reached by the A32 or the A334

THE PUB Greens Restaurant & Pub, The Square, Wixkham. Tel: 01329 833197

❶ Take care on the short section of the route which follws the busy A32.

■ TOURIST INFORMATION CENTRES

Fareham
Westbury Manor,
84 West Street.
Tel: 01329 221342

Portsmouth
Clarence Esplanade,
Southsea.
Tel: 023 9282 6722

Southampton
9 Civic Centre Road.
Tel: 023 8083 3333;
www.visit-southampton.co.uk

■ PLACES OF INTEREST

Bursledon Brickworks
Swanwick Lane, Swanwick.
Tel: 01489 576248

Bursledon Windmill
Windmill Lane, Bursledon.
Tel: 0845 603 5635;
www.hants.gov.uk/museum/
windmill

Charles Dickens' Birthplace
393 Old Commercial Road,
Portsmouth.
Tel: 023 9282 7261;
www.charlesdickensbirth
place.co.uk

City Museum & Art Gallery
Museum Road, Portsmouth.
Tel: 023 9282 7261;
www.portsmouthcity
museums.co.uk

Cumberland House Natural History Museum
Eastern Parade, Southsea.
Tel: 023 9282 7261;
www.chnhm.co.uk
Free.

D-Day Museum & Overlord Embroidery
Clarence Esplanade,
Southsea. Tel: 023 9282 7261;
www.ddaymuseum.co.uk

Explosion! Museum of Naval Firepower
Priddy's Hard, Gosport.
Tel: 023 9250 5600;
www.explosion.org.uk

Hawthorns Urban Wildlife Centre
Southampton Common.
Tel: 023 8067 1921;
www. southampton.gov.uk
Free.

Manor Farm Country Park & Farm Museum
Pylands Lane, Bursledon.
Tel: 01489 787055;
www.hants.gov.uk/manorfarm

Maritime Museum
Town Quay, Southampton.
Tel: 023 8063 5904;
www.southampton.gov.uk
Free.

Netley Abbey (EH)
Tel: 023 8045 5157. Free.

Portchester Castle (EH)
Castle Street, Portchester.
Tel: 0239 237 8291

Portsmouth Historic Dockyard
Victory Gate, HM Naval Base.
Tel: 023 9286 1512/9766;
www.historicdockyard.co.uk

Royal Armouries
Fort Nelson, Portsdown Hill
Road, Fareham.
Tel: 01329 233734;
www.royalarmouries.org

Royal Marines Museum
Southsea.
Tel: 023 9281 9385; www.
royalmarinesmuseum.co.uk

Royal Navy Submarine Museum
Haslar Jetty Road, Gosport.
Tel: 023 9251 0345;
www.rnsubmus.co.uk

Royal Victoria Country Park
Tel: 023 8045 5157; www.
hants.gov.uk/rvcp

Southampton City Art Gallery
Civic Centre.
Tel: 023 8083 2277;
www.southampton.gov.uk/art

Southsea Castle Museum
Clarence Esplanade.
Tel: 023 9282 7261;
www.southseacastle.co.uk

Spinnaker Tower
Gunwharf Quays,
Portsmouth.
Tel: 02392 857520;
www.spinnakertower.co.uk

Titchfield Haven National Nature Reserve
Hill Head, by Stubbington.
Tel: 01329 662145;
www.hants.gov.uk/titchfield

Wickham Vineyard
Botley Road, Shedfield.
Tel: 01329 834042;
www.wickhamvineyard.co.uk

■ FOR CHILDREN

Blue Reef Aquarium
Clarence Esplanade,
Southsea.
Tel: 023 9287 5222;
www.bluereefaquarium.co.uk

The Pyramids Centre
Clarence Esplanade,
Southsea.
Tel: 023 9279 9977;
www.pyramids.co.uk

■ SHOPPING
Bargate Markets
Bargate, Southampton.
Friday market, plus Farmers'
Markets one Sat per month
(www.hampshirefarmers
markets.co.uk). There are
artists' markets on the first
and third Sat each month
Gunwharf Quays
www.gunwharf-quays.com
**The Mall Marlands
Shopping Centre**
Civic Centre Road,
Southampton.
Tel: 023 8033 9164;
www.themall.co.uk
West Quay Shopping Centre
Tel: 023 8033 6828;
www.west-quay.co.uk
**Whiteley Village Outlet
Shopping**
Close to junction 9, M27.
www.whiteleyvillage.com

■ PERFORMING ARTS
Kings Theatre
Albert Road, Southsea.
Tel: 023 92 828282
www.kings-southsea.com
The Mayflower
Commercial Road,
Southampton.
Tel: 023 8071 1811
www.the-mayflower.com

New Theatre Royal
20–24 Guildhall Walk,
Portsmouth.
Tel: 023 9264 9000;
www.newtheatreroyal.com
Nuffield Theatre
University Road,
Southampton.
Tel: 023 8067 1771

■ SPORTS & ACTIVITIES
BOAT TRIPS
Blue Funnel Cruises
Ocean Village, Southampton.
Tel: 023 8022 3278;
www.bluefunnel.co.uk
SS *Shieldhall*
47 Berth, Eastern Dock,
Dock Gate 4, Southampton,
Tel: 023 8022 3278;
www.ss-shieldhall.co.uk
HORSE-RIDING
**Gleneagles
Equestrian Centre**
Allington Lane, West End,
Southampton.
Tel: 023 8047 3370
WALKING
The Solent Way
A 60-mile (96km) long-
distance walk from Milford on
Sea to Emsworth.
Hayling Billy Trail
A 4-mile (6km) trail between
Havant and Langston.
The Strawberry Trail
15-mile (24km) circular walk
in the Hamble Valley.

■ ANNUAL CUSTOMS & EVENTS
Botley
Summer Festival, end Jun.
Hamble Week
Carnival week, early Jul.
Tel: 023 8045 7935;
www.hambleevents.org.uk
Netley
Fireworks Spectacular, Royal
Victoria Country Park, around
5 Nov. Tel: 023 8045 5157
Netley Marsh Steam
& Craft Show
Mid-Jul. Meadow Mead Farm.
Tel: 023 8086 7882;
www.netleymarshsteamand
craftshow.org
Southampton
Kite Festival, mid-Jun at
Lordshill.
**The Big Southampton
Boat Show**
Mid-Sep. Tel: 0844 209 0333
**Swanwick, Bursledon
and Warsash Regatta**
Around Elephant Boatyard,
end Aug.
Tel: 023 8045 6969;
www.bursledonregatta.co.uk
Titchfield
Carnival and bonfire, last Mon
in Oct.

Tea Rooms

Lilly's Tea & Coffee House

The Square, Wickham
PO17 5JT. Tel: 01329 830305;
www.lillyswickham.com
You're spoiled for choice here
– the three-tier afternoon tea
is a delight and the cake and
cupcake selection is
impressive. Milkshakes and
sundaes are on the menu.

The Pantry Tea Room

Manor Farm Country Park,
Pylands Lane, Bursledon
SO30 2ER. Tel: 01489 787055
In a perfect rural setting of
this old farmstead, tuck into a
snack, ice cream or a full-
blown, home-cooked meal.

Tower Café Bar

Spinnaker Tower, Gunwharf
Quays, Portsmouth PO1 3TT
Tel: 02392 857520;
www.spinnakertower.co.uk
Take your morning coffee or
afternoon tea in style in
Portsmouth's signature
tower. Sandwiches and cakes
give way to wine and beer in
the evenings, as you sit and
watch the sun go down.

Deli Adriano

Shore Road, Warsash
SO31 9GQ
Tel: 01489 577762
www.deliadriano.biz
This superb deli and coffee
shop is an absolute treat.
The deli sells cured meats,
smoked fish, olives, organic
fruit and vegetables and fresh
bread as well as home-made
biscuits and cakes. The coffee
shop sells wonderful coffee
as well as cakes, soups,
panini and more substantial
lunchtime dishes such as
lasagne or beef stew

Pubs

The Cowherds

The Common, Southampton
SO15 7NN
Tel: 023 8055 8405
On the A33, at the heart of
Southampton Common, this
pub was once the haunt of
cattle drovers on their way to
London. Now it's the perfect
spot for lunch or dinner – try
the ham hock with mustard
sauce, or perhaps the pork,
apple and cider sausages
with Cheddar mash. There's a
patio outside and inside it's
cosy with open fires, oak
beams and wood panelling.

Greens Restaurant & Pub

The Square, Wickham
PO17 5JQ
Tel: 01329 833197;
www.greenrestaurant.co.uk
Set on a corner of Wickham's
picturesque square, and
close to the River Meon, the
menus at this mock-Tudor
pub make good use of fresh
ingredients, from smoked
duck salad with pear chutney
to delicious apricot-glazed
bread-and-butter pudding.
Food is not served on
Mondays. Beers include
Hopback Summer Lightning
and Fullers London Pride.

The Jolly Sailor

Lands End Road, Burseldon
SO31 8DN
Tel: 023 8040 5557
This appealing old pub,
overlooking Hamble marina,
achieved fame in the 1980s as
a location for BBC TV's salty
soap opera, *Howard's Way*.
The menus include a variety
of offerings, from *moules
marinière* and *bouillabaisse* to
chunky sandwiches. Beers
include Fursty Ferret and
Tanglefoot.

The Still & West

2 Bath Square, Old
Portsmouth PO1 2JL
Tel: 023 9282 1567
At the top of Broad Street,
and close to HMS *Victory*, this
nautically themed 1504 pub
has great views over the
harbour and to the Isle of
Wight. As you might expect,
there's lots of fish on the
menu, including a trademark
grill of fresh fish and
mussels, and of course, fish
and chips.

Winchester & Salisbury

Winchester, England's ancient capital, lies amid rolling chalkland scenery, with roads radiating outwards from it across the county. Surrounding it, particularly to the north and west, are two contrasting landscapes: the wide serene chalklands of 'High Hampshire', lonely and open, dotted here and there with clumps of dark green yews and graceful beeches, and the fisherman's Hampshire – shallow green valleys of water meadows and sparkling streams that bring anglers from the four winds to try their skill in England's most famous trout rivers. This is an area of unhurried little roads, great houses and gardens, tranquil rivers and sweeping views.

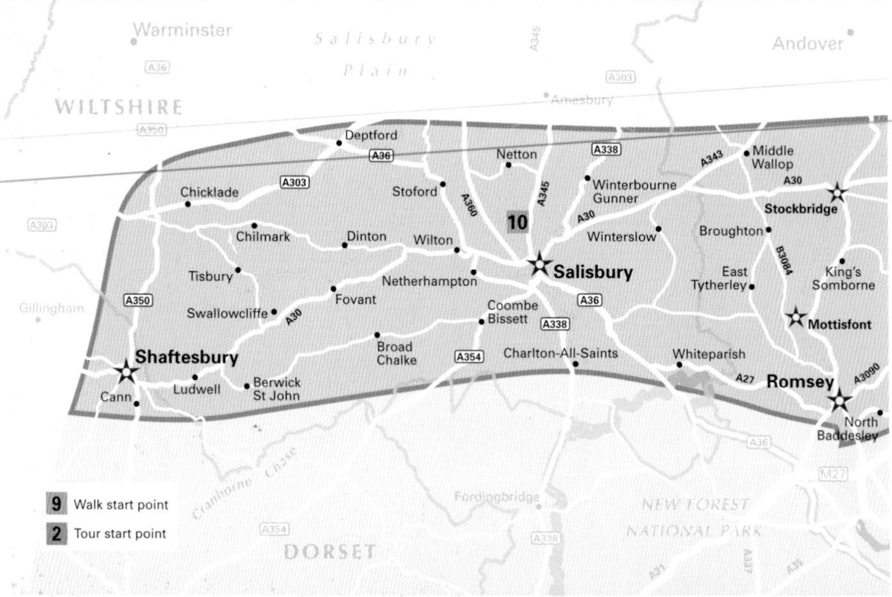

9 Walk start point

2 Tour start point

RIVER TEST

HAMPSHIRE

A34
A203

A30
A34
A33
Micheldever
Swarraton
Kings
Worthy
M3
New
Alresford
A31
Winchester 2
Avington
Park
9
B3049
Farley
Mount
Cheriton
Hinton
Ampner
Hursley
A272
A32
Twyford
Warnford
Ampfield
Colden
Common
Upham
SOUTH DOWNS
Corhampton
Eastleigh
NATIONAL PARK
(proposed)
Southampton
M27
A334
Waterlooville

Unmissable attractions

Stroll in lovely Hillier Gardens, where you will witness a blaze of colour whatever the season...gain an insight into the life of Lord Mountbatten at Broadlands magnificent mansion...savour the haunting atmosphere of Salisbury Cathedral as you listen to the pure harmonies of its choir...test your stamina by climbing Shaftesbury's much-photographed and filmed, cobbled Gold Hill...admire the grandeur of Mottisfont Abbey...amble beside the sparkling watercress beds in Alresford...fly-fish for trout on the River Test then retreat to The Mayfly to swap stories of 'the one that got away'...visit the cathedral city of Winchester, steeped in historical fact and folklore.

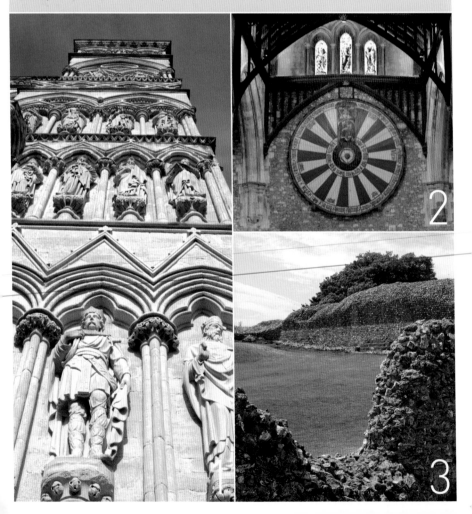

1 Salisbury Cathedral
Building work on the cathedral began in 1220; an army of labourers and craftsmen toiled for around 40 years. The tower and famous spire were added in the 14th century.

2 Great Hall, Winchester
The only remaining intact part of Winchester Castle now houses the top of a painted table. Once claimed as King Arthur's famous Round Table, tests have shown that it probably dates from Tudor times.

3 Old Sarum
William the Conqueror erected a castle here soon after his arrival in England. Eventually a cathedral was built in the grounds but in the 13th century this was moved to nearby Salisbury.

4 Watercress Line
The great days of steam rail travel have been revived on this line which runs between Alresford and Alton. When constructed in the mid-19th century, the line ran from Winchester to Alton. The track and trains are maintained by enthusiastic volunteers.

5 Hillier Gardens
Sir Harold Hillier established his arboretum in 1953 in the grounds of his home. The stunning plant collection extends over 180 acres (72ha).

ALRESFORD MAP REF SU3832

Lovely Alresford, with its wide streets of friendly Georgian houses of brick and stucco, lies in the broad valley of the River Alre, hence the name (pronounced 'Allsford'). It is really two places – Old Alresford to the north of the river, which is now no more than a village with an adjoining park, and New Alresford, the busy market town to the south which was 'New' in about 1200. Between the two is Alresford Pond, created by Bishop de Lucy in the 13th century. Its dam, the Great Weir, is the largest non-military medieval earthwork in England and the only one that still serves this original dual purpose of dam and road causeway. Today its 30 acres (12ha) are a haven for wildlife and also feed the famous local watercress beds.

New Alresford retains its medieval street plan, with a T-shape formed by the spacious elegant Broad Street and West and East Streets, the old Winchester–London road. A borough by 1294, New Alresford soon became one of England's ten greatest wool markets. Two of its mills survive, the Town Mill and the old Fulling Mill. Fires devastated New Alresford between the early 15th century and 1689, which accounts for its mainly Georgian appearance.

Approach from Old Alresford or from Bishop's Sutton for the most attractive introduction to the town – the south approach from Cheriton leads through less inviting modern suburbs. Strolling through New Alresford is a delight. The town has a variety of interesting shops and some excellent craft workshops, and Broad Street, with its line of lime trees and pretty old fashioned lamps, is one of Hampshire's finest streets.

Mary Russell Mitford, author of the classic *Our Village*, was born at 27 Broad Street in 1787 and lived there until she was ten, when she moved with her father to Three Mile Cross near Reading – the village of her book. She later wrote, 'Alresford is or will be celebrated in history for two things: the first, to speak modestly, is my birth, the second is cricket'. Few today would associate Alresford with cricket, but Taylor of Alresford, a member of the famous Hambledon Club was born here, and cricket writer and commentator John Arlott once lived at the Old Sun. Today Alresford is better known for its watercress beds and its steam railway, the Watercress Line.

North of Alresford, Northington Grange is the dramatic empty shell of a neoclassical mansion, where the 1999 movie *Onegin* was filmed.

■ Insight

HAMPSHIRE WATERCRESS

Watercress needs to be planted to remain submerged in gently flowing shallow water if it is to be grown to perfection, and few places have exactly the right conditions. The Hampshire chalklands with their sparkling streams fit the bill precisely, particularly around Alresford where the plants flourish in specially constructed beds alongside the streams. Watercress needs to be consumed soon after it is picked because it wilts easily; the Watercress Line, now a preserved steam railway, originally carried the harvest to London markets; today container lorries transport it to the European market.

AMPFIELD MAP REF SU4023

In rolling countryside to the southwest of Winchester, this little village, set among beech woods and vast cornfields, is best known for the nearby Hillier Gardens. Sir Harold Hillier, the great plantsman, began his famous collection of trees and shrubs on the Ampfield estate in 1953. It became one of the largest in the world, with some 40,000 temperate plants originating from every continent. There is colour at every season of the year with witch hazels, rhododendrons, autumn foliage and herbaceous perennials.

The heart of the village is at Knapp, now designated a conservation area. There were clay pits and a pottery near by, and the well-known Potters Heron Hotel preserves in its name a shadowy recollection of the old industry, since a potter's treadle wheel is also known as a 'hern' or 'heron'. In much later times this same clay was used to make the bricks for the Church of St Mark, built between 1838 and 1841 at the instigation of John Keble, a famous member of the High Church Oxford Movement, who was vicar at nearby Hursley.

Ampfield has literary associations. Richard Morley, the 17th-century 'Hedge Poet', lived here and the Rev W Awdry, author of the 'Thomas the Tank Engine' books, spent his boyhood in Ampfield, where his father was the vicar.

AVINGTON PARK

MAP REF SU5432

Avington Park lies between Easton and Alresford, east of Winchester. Dating mainly to the early 18th century, but with some parts much earlier, it is a

■ Insight

ROYAL ASSIGNATIONS

Avington Park's owner, George Brydges, had as his patron no less a personage than Charles II. The king and his mistress, Nell Gwynn, would stay at Avington during the six weeks of Winchester's horse racing season. More royal assignations were reputed to have taken place here about 150 years later, when George IV would enjoy private meetings with his mistress, Mrs Fitzherbert.

big rose-pink house with a splendid portico and some wonderful interior features, including a painted ceiling by Verrio and a fine colonnade in the 19th-century conservatory. In November 1825 William Cobbett rode through on his way from Easton, and described the scene: '...The house is close down at the edge of the meadow land; there is a lawn before it, and a pond supplied by the Itchen...We looked down on all this from a rising ground, and the water, like a looking-glass, showed us the trees, and even the animals. This certainly is one of the prettiest spots in the world...' The views to the house across the lake and parkland seem little changed.

The brick-built Church of St Mary was built in from 1768 to 1771 by Margaret, Marchioness of Carnarvon. It preserves the air of the 18th century as verily as the view over the park. A large monument to the Marchioness, who died in 1768, is in pink and white marble with two urns and an obelisk. Another monument is to John Shelley, brother of the famous poet, who purchased Avington Park in 1847.

A walk around the Alresfords

New Alresford is one of Hampshire's most picturesque small towns. Much of the architecture is Georgian, and a stroll around the three principal streets reveals a traditional country town shops plus specialist clothes, antiquarian books and craft shops. Close to both Old and New Alresford you will find a network of crystal clear chalk streams, rivulets and channels that form the rivers Arle and Itchen and the Candover Stream. Since Victorian times these springs and rivers have played a vital role in the production of watercress making Alresford the 'Watercress Capital' of England, and the steam railway once transported watercress across the country.

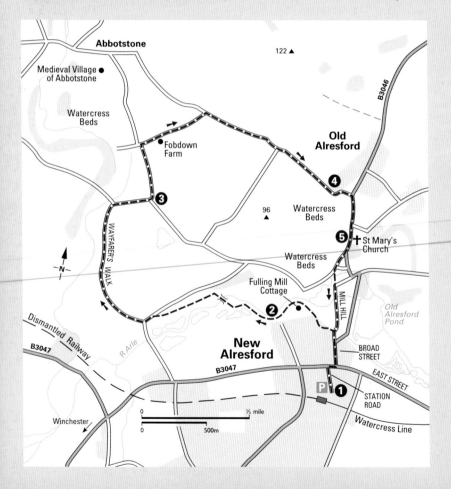

Route Directions

1 From the car park walk down Station Road to the T-junction with West Street. Turn right, then left down Broad Street and keep left at the bottom along Mill Hill. Half way down turn left into Ladywell Lane and soon join the river bank and pass the attractive, timbered and thatched Fulling Mill Cottage which straddles the River Arle.

2 Continue to the bottom of Dean Lane and keep to the riverside path. Cross a footbridge over the river, and ascend to pass some cottages. Shortly, a lane merges from your right; follow it for 50yds (46m), then fork right onto the Wayfarer's Walk and continue to a junction of tracks. Bear right uphill to a lane.

3 Turn left, descend to Fobdown Farm and take the track on the right beside the farm buildings. On reaching a T-junction of tracks, turn right and follow the established track for just over 0.5mile (800m), gently descending into Old Alresford.

4 Pass watercress beds on your right and follow the now metalled lane left, past houses. Turn right beside the green to reach the B3046. Cross over and follow the pavement right to a lane opposite St Mary's Church.

5 Having visited the church, cross the road and turn left along the pavement to a grass triangle by a junction. Bear right along the lane and take the footpath ahead over a stream and beside watercress beds back to Mill Hill and Broad Street.

Route facts

DISTANCE/TIME
4 miles (6.4km) 2h

MAP OS Explorer 132 Winchester

START Pay car park off Station Road, New Alresford, grid ref: SU 588325

TRACKS Riverside paths, tracks, field, woodland paths and roads

GETTING TO THE START New Alresford is signposted off the A31 between Winchester and Alton, 6 miles (9.7km) east of Winchester. On the main village street, follow signs to the Watercress Line to locate the parking area.

THE PUB The Globe on the Lake, The Soke, Broad Street, Alresford. Tel: 01962 732294; www.globeonthelake.co.uk

❶ Alresford can be busy with cars; some riverside paths; take care crossing the B3046. Suitable for all ages.

■ Insight

THE SILVER ROUTE

The Roman road from the Mendip mines via Old Sarum and Winchester crosses Farley Mount. This road was once used to transport the precious silver-bearing lead to Bitterne, now a suburb of Southampton, for shipment to the Roman Imperial Mint at Lyon. Today, this important road can be traced eastwards as an embankment under the trees, but once you get nearer to Winchester it is followed by the present-day Sarum Road.

FARLEY MOUNT MAP REF SU4029

Farley Mount Country Park covers over 1,000 acres (405ha) of chalk upland west of Winchester and east of the broad Test valley. At 586 feet (178m), it remains the highest point in the region and there are wonderful views in all directions. Its most prominent feature is the pyramid folly, a memorial raised in 1734 to a horse who bravely won its race despite having fallen into a chalk pit while out hunting the previous day. The horse was renamed Beware Chalk Pit.

This popular country park is best known for its variety of habitats, with short turf, mixed woodland and Forestry Commission plantation. There is plenty of wildlife in the old oak, beech and yew woods and also in the great swathes of ancient coppicing. Orchids are plentiful and there are a number of nature trails in Crab Wood, on the east side of the park. Car parks are clearly marked. The park is crossed by the Roman road from the Mendip silver-lead mines and Old Sarum to Winchester, and by the Clarendon Way long-distance footpath.

MOTTISFONT MAP REF SU3226

The little village of Mottisfont lies in that part of the wide green Test valley where the trees seem to be exceptionally large, the streams of the river are particularly numerous and the atmosphere breathes peace and prosperity. The village's name is derived from the spring or 'font' which rises where the village 'moot' was held in Saxon times.

A house of Augustinian canons was founded here in 1201, which at the Dissolution passed to Lord Sandys, in exchange for the then villages of Paddington and Chelsea. Unusually, it was the church that he converted into his mansion, demolishing the residential parts of the priory. The Tudor building was remodelled in the 18th century by the Mills family, to whom it had passed, giving rise to the present mellow house.

Today Mottisfont Abbey (National Trust) is famed for its drawing room, decorated in Gothic trompe l'oeil style by Rex Whistler in 1938, and for Derek Hill's 20th-century picture collection. The tranquil grounds have sweeping lawns which run down to the River Test. The walled garden houses the National Collection of old roses, superb in June.

ROMSEY MAP REF SU3521

This small town on the River Test is dominated by its magnificent Abbey Church of 1120–70, a handsome Norman building with a low, square tower, massive walls, a splendid south doorway and an interior of beautifully carved Norman arches. It contains two remarkable Saxon stone carvings from earlier churches on the site, and its treasures include the Romsey Psalter (a 15th-century illuminated manuscript), and a monument to the noted economist Sir William Petty (1623–87), born in Romsey and a founder member of the Royal Society. Lord Mountbatten of Burma (1900–79), one-time confidant to Prince Charles, is buried in the abbey.

Romsey is an attractive place with many unobtrusively pleasing streets of Georgian and later houses. It centres on spacious Market Place, which has a statue in the middle of Lord Palmerston, the Victorian statesman who lived at Broadlands. The 13th-century timbered King John's House, opposite the Abbey Church, is said to be where John's daughter lived before she married the Scottish king. There is a lovely park with a bandstand, beside the River Test.

Across the river are the gates of Broadlands, a Palladian mansion with a great 18th-century portico, set in a landscaped park that was created by 'Capability' Brown. Once the home of Lord Palmerston, more recently of Lord Mountbatten and now of Lord Romsey, it houses exhibitions on Mountbatten's life and a spectacular Mountbatten audiovisual presentation in the stable block. The house contains many fine works of art including several pieces by Van Dyck. Rooms include the stately Saloon and a powder-blue Wedgwood Room. Furniture by Ince and Mayhew was made specifically for the house.

To the east, the churchyard of East Wellow contains the grave of Florence Nightingale (1820–1910), the founder of modern nursing. The church has some unusual 13th-century wall paintings.

■ **Visit**

ROMSEY ABBEY

The nuns of Romsey Abbey were almost wiped out by the Black Death, and after the Dissolution the church was purchased by the people of Romsey who, until then, had worshipped under sufferance in the north transept. We must be grateful to those Tudor townsfolk who raised the necessary £100 to buy the church, since not only Hampshire but all England would be the poorer without this wonderful parish church, the largest in the county.

■ **Visit**

CATHEDRAL CHOIR

There has been a choir at Salisbury Cathedral for around 800 years, and today it is famous for admitting girls as well as boys. Children as young as seven years old can join the choir school, taking part in regular lessons alongside their daily two singing practices. Hear them during term time at evensong and at special services throughout the year.

SALISBURY MAP REF SU1530

Old Sarum's history dates back to a time long before records were made, and the giant earthwork is founded on an Iron Age camp that covered around 56 acres (23ha). The earliest settlers were followed by Romans, Anglo-Saxons, Danes and Norman – William the Conqueror is said to have reviewed his troops here in 1070.

A Norman castle and cathedral were erected, but water was scarce on this plain, and the military and ecclesiastical factions could not agree who should take precedence. Accordingly, in 1220 a new cathedral was planned to the south in nearby New Sarum – or Salisbury – using stones from the old one. It seems that the spirit went out of Old Sarum in more ways than one, as the castle fell into decay, and the town was gradually abandoned. There's not much to see of this once-thriving settlement today, but for the excavated foundations of the old cathedral and fragments of the castle.

And so, while Winchester's old heart may seem like a medieval muddle, Salisbury feels comparatively spacious and regular – it was planned and built on a grid structure, beside the River Avon. Many old streets are named after the goods that were sold there – Fish Row, Butchers Row, and so on. Some have been pedestrianised, and highlights to look out for include the 16th-century façade of the Joiner's Hall on St Ann Street and the 18th-century Guildhall. The Poultry Cross in Silver Street dates to the 15th century.

Unusually, the Gothic cathedral was built in almost one go, the majority of it being completed by 1258, at a cost of around £27,000. The main exception is its soaring spire, 404 feet (123m) high, which was added in the 14th century and is the structure's most identifiable feature, painted most memorably by John Constable from across the water meadows in 1823. A climb up 332 steps and through the cathedral's roof spaces takes you to the top of the tower for far-reaching views over the city and around.

Salisbury cathedral's interior was unfortunately drastically remodelled in the 18th century by James Wyatt, who 'decluttered' it by clearing screens and tombs and throwing out some of the old stained glass. Wyatt also covered over the 13th-century roof painting in the choir, but this was later restored. Today the most striking glass is the intense blue 'Prisoners of Conscience Window' in the Trinity Chapel.

Two of the cathedral's most prized possessions are the clock of 1386, the oldest in England, and an original copy of the Magna Carta, the 'great document' forced by rebellious barons on King John at Runnymede in 1215, to limit the monarch's more arbitrary powers. It's surprisingly small for such a significant document, about A3 size.

A stroll around the cathedral close is essential, including gracious old houses such as the Old Deanery, and the King's House, now home to the interesting Salisbury and South Wiltshire Museum, which includes finds from Stonehenge, watercolours by Turner, history relating to Old Sarum, and the Warminster Jewel. Mompesson House is a gem in Queen Anne style, with notable plasterwork and a pretty walled garden. It played a starring role in the 1995 film of Jane Austen's *Sense and Sensibility*. The Wardrobe has a military museum.

The 17th-century Palladian mansion of Wilton House, home of the Earl of Pembroke, lies west of the town, and is well worth a look for its famous Single and Double Cube Rooms and its elegant gardens. The house was also the most unlikely setting for the D-Day landings headquarters during the Second World War; more recently, scenes from *Sense and Sensibility*, *The Madness of King George*, *Mrs Brown* and the 2005 movie *Pride and Prejudice* were filmed here.

Winchester to Salisbury

This circular route links the historic centres of Winchester and Salisbury, with their fine cathedrals, and the market towns of Stockbridge and Romsey, set deep in the beautiful Test Valley. The drive takes you through rolling countryside and passes many pretty villages. Along the way you will pass some of the area's most attractive houses and gardens, and if you have time, it's worth stopping at one or two places to stretch your legs and appreciate all that these magnificent homes have to offer.

Route Directions

1 Leave the centre of Winchester, following signs for Romsey and the A3090. Pass the hospital, go straight on at a roundabout, and bear right at the next, signed to Romsey. Pass a golf course, left, go through Pitt and down a long hill, to turn right just before the village of Standon, signed to 'Farley Mount and Sparsholt'. Very soon turn left, signed Farley Mount, and follow this narrow country lane through trees to the open hilltops for 2 miles (3km) to reach Farley Mount Country Park. Keep left.
There are several car parks on your right where you can stop and visit the country park. The folly monument is up to your left.

2 The road descends steadily through beautiful chalky landscape. Go through the pretty village of Ashley with its white-painted church and old well. Bear left at the end of the village for King's Somborne and Romsey. At the

next junction bear left, and go through the village of King's Somborne with its pretty thatched houses. Turn right at the end, and right again in front of the Crown Inn onto the A3057. Follow this for 3 miles (4.8km) to a junction on the edge of Stockbridge and turn left at the roundabout, signed 'Salisbury'. Go through Stockbridge, cross the River Test and immediately turn left on a minor road, signed 'Houghton.' This road runs largely parallel with the river. The village of Houghton is long and spread out. Look out for Houghton Lodge, on your left, with its glorious gardens and lawns sweeping down to the River Test.

3 Continue past the black-and-white timbered Boot Inn. After 2.5 miles (4km) reach a junction. Turn right for Dunbridge, and keep going straight ahead for Mottisfont. Continue on this narrow road through rolling farmland into

Mottisfont village. Go straight on through to visit the famous Abbey and gardens.
In a picturesque setting by the River Test, Mottisfont Abbey is adapted from a 12th-century priory. In the gardens are the National Collection of old-fashioned roses.

4 Retrace your route through the village and turn left on Bengers Lane, signed to Dunbridge and Broughton. At the junction with the B3084 turn left down Hatt Hill and go downhill into Dunbridge. Cross the river and railway line and turn right, signed to Lockerley. At the junction in Lockerley turn right, signed 'East Tytherley', pass under the railway and then turn left after the church, for East and West Dean. Pass through Lockerley Green.
The hamlet of Lockerley Green is built around a large village green.

5 Cross the railway, pass through East Dean village,

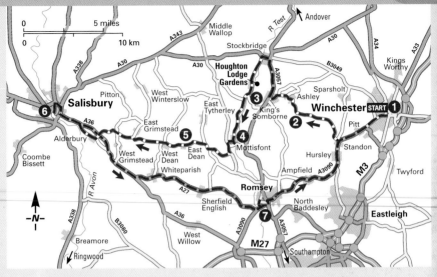

and West Dean with its
lumber yard and thatched
cottages. Turn left by the old
brick bridge, signed 'East
Grimstead and Salisbury'.
Go straight ahead at the
junction for East Grimstead,
then go under the railway
and soon you enter East
Grimstead, with its neat
little flint church. Turn left,
signed 'West Grimstead and
Salisbury', and keep straight
on this road, proceeding
through wooded Alderbury.
At the junction turn right
for Salisbury, and continue
downhill to meet the A36.
Turn left and follow this into
the middle of Salisbury,
following signs round the ring
road to the Central Car Park.
Explore the medieval city on
foot taking in the cathedral
and the museums that are

housed in some of the historic
buildings in Cathedral Close.

6 Leave Salisbury on the A36,
signed to Southampton. Once
you get to the end of
the dual carriageway, look
out for the viewpoint of
Pepperbox Hill to your left.
Descend to traffic lights and
turn left on the A27, signed
to Romsey and Whiteparish.
Pass through Whiteparish,
with its handsome old
houses, and a string of
hamlets that follow including
Sherfield English. Look out
for the bulky Abbey on your
left as you descend further
towards Romsey. At the
junction turn left, signed
'Romsey and Winchester'.
Cross the River Test
and, when you reach the
roundabout by Broadlands,

make a left turn to Romsey
town centre.
In Romsey, visit King John's
Hunting Lodge, now a
heritage centre, and pick up
a copy of a town trail to assist
your exploration.

7 Return to the Broadlands
roundabout and turn left
for Winchester. Stay on the
A3090, passing a turning on
the left for Hillier Gardens.
Continue through Ampfield
and Hursley, a blend of real
and mock-Tudor, to Standon.
Now retrace your morning
route back into the centre of
Winchester.

Old Sarum

This walk explores the Avon Valley and fortified Old Sarum – the massive, deserted ramparts and earthworks set on a bleak hill overlooking modern-day Salisbury (New Sarum). Old Sarum was an important royal and ecclesiastical site, with a castle erected on an earlier Iron Age hill-fort. A cathedral was built inside the castle grounds, but moved to Salisbury in the 13th century.

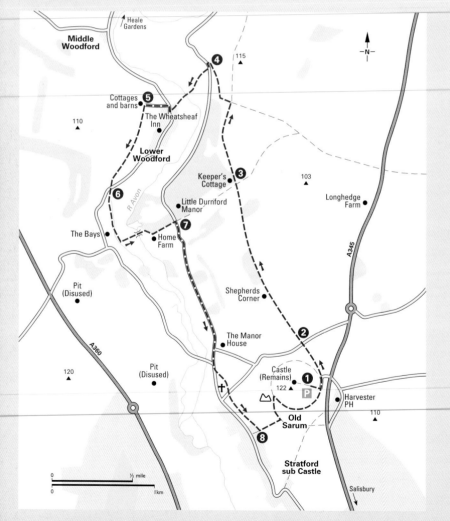

Route Directions

1 From the car park, walk down the access road through the outer bank of the fortified site. Bear left; then, as the road bends right, go through the two gates leading to a waymarked and fenced bridle path and follow this until you reach a road.

2 Go through the gate opposite and follow the track ahead. Pass a cottage (Shepherds Corner) and ascend the track. In 0.25 mile (400m), descend to Keeper's Cottage and reach a crossing of paths.

3 Keep straight on, heading uphill and between fields into a wooded area. At a crossing of bridle paths, turn left and descend a tree-lined path. At a boundary marker, bear right and continue to a road.

4 Turn left, then right in 50yds (46m) down a metalled lane. Cross the River Avon and two further footbridges, then follow the metalled path and drive to a road. Turn left for The Wheatsheaf Inn; otherwise, turn right and in 50yds (46m) turn left up a lane.

5 Just before cottages and barns, turn left over a stile and walk down the left-hand field-edge, crossing two more stiles and fields. Maintain direction across the next field, cross a track and go through the hedge ahead, then in 100yds (91m) reach a road.

6 Cross the road diagonally and take the path down a wooded track. Pass to the left of 'The Bays' to a stile and turn right between the stream and fence. Cross double stiles in the corner and turn sharp left over a stile and turn right beside the stream to a white gate and a metalled drive. Turn left and skirt Home Farm and Little Durnford Manor to a gate and road.

7 Turn right and follow the road for 0.75 mile (1.2km) to a staggered crossroads. Keep ahead towards Salisbury, crossing the stile on your left in 100yds (91m). Bear half-left across the field, then skirt the churchyard to reach a stile, a metalled path and a further stile. Head down the next field, cross a stile and pass a barn, then cross a stile on to a fenced track.

8 Turn left uphill towards the tree-covered ramparts. Keep left at the junction of paths by a gate, then fork right through a gate and climb on to the outer rampart. Turn right and follow the path to a gate and Old Sarum's access road. Turn left back to the car park.

Route facts

DISTANCE/TIME
6 miles (9.7km) 2h

MAP OS Explorer 130 Salisbury & Stonehenge

START English Heritage car park (closes 6pm; 4pm winter), grid ref: SU 139326

TRACKS Footpaths, tracks, bridle paths, stretches of road, 10 stiles

GETTING TO THE START Old Sarum is north of Salisbury off the A345.

THE PUB The Wheatsheaf Inn, Lower Woodford. Tel: 01722 782203

SHAFTESBURY MAP REF ST8723

The idyllic view from the top of Gold Hill in Shaftesbury, with the line of cottages tipping down the steep cobbled road ahead and a perfect panorama of rolling green Dorset hills behind, is one of the best known in England. You are bound to have seen it before – it is used as the backdrop of many a TV period costume drama, and most famously at the centre of the 1970s Hovis bread advertisements on television, revived in 2006. In fact, thanks in part to the publicity generated by the original Hovis ads, the cobbled road and 700-year-old buttressed abbey walls opposite were given a much needed restoration and makeover in 1980. Today it is a totally pedestrian zone and genuinely charming despite all the hype, though your knees may complain of the steepness after a walk down and back.

The abbey was founded in AD 888, on the edge of Cranborne Chase, by King Alfred for his daughter Aethelgifu and a community of Benedictine nuns. Edward the Martyr, murdered at Corfe Castle, was buried here in 979, making it a very popular (as well as prosperous) site of pilgrimage, and the Danish King Canute insisted that his heart should be interred in the abbey after his death in 1035. In 1539 it was abandoned as part of the Dissolution of Monasteries that took place across England, and today you can stroll around the low ruins, admire the remains of the Abbey Church, and learn more at the associated museum with its large Anglo Saxon herb garden.

Shaftesbury Town Museum stands at the top of Gold Hill, and celebrates this historic market town which grew fat on the profits of cereals and dairy produce from Cranborne Chase and the near by Blackmore Vale (and the town still fills up for Thursday markets). Traditional Dorsetshire bonnets and button-making were two of the small-scale industries of the town in years gone by.

Just off Bell Street, Swan's Yard is home to many local craftspeople and artists, and is well worth exploring. Another favourite corner is the Pump Yard, near the Olde Two Brewers Inn. It's a delightful little private courtyard of restored houses facing onto St James Street, with an old pump at the centre.

STOCKBRIDGE MAP REF SU3635

Lying deep in the broad Test valley, and spanning that many-streamed river on an artificial causeway constructed in Roman times, Stockbridge consists of a gracious wide street lined with an attractive variety of little houses and shops, with open views eastwards to the hills. It feels as if it should be the main thoroughfare of a sizeable town, but it is not, and behind the elegant façades, the gift and antiques shops, the art galleries and the hotels are the water meadows of the River Test. Some of the river's streamlets, teeming with trout, flow under and alongside the main street.

The most prestigious of English angling clubs, The Houghton, has its headquarters at the Grosvenor Hotel, Stockbridge's most impressive building, with a great pillared porch that juts out into the street and a room above. The town was on a main drovers' route between Wales and Surrey and Kent, and sheep fairs were held here from Tudor times until the early 20th century. Stockbridge Common Marsh is ancient land in the care of the National Trust, as is the open Stockbridge Down, where there is a large Bronze Age cemetery consisting of 15 round barrows.

Northwest of Stockbridge, on the A343, is the Museum of Army Flying at Middle Wallop airfield, which celebrates the history of army aviation. Exhibits include an Argentine Huey helicopter, captured during the Falklands War, and there are hands-on games and activities especially for children.

WINCHESTER MAP REF SU4829

Physically, Winchester is relatively small. Spiritually, emotionally and historically it is large indeed. It was founded shortly before the Romans came, at an important crossing point of the River Itchen. A glance at a map shows how Roman roads radiate from the city like the spokes of a wheel, and certainly Roman Winchester – Venta Belgarum – was as important as this road pattern suggests.

Winchester declined when the Romans left, so that when the shires were created in the 8th century, it did not give its name to the new county. Within a century the situation had been reversed and 'Vintanceastir', as Bede called it, was again ascendant. Alfred the Great made it capital of the West Saxons in AD 871 – Hamo Thorneycroft's statue of him stands at the foot of the High Street – and Winchester remained the capital of Wessex and, in a sense, of England, well into Norman times.

■ Visit

OLD WARDOUR
Northeast of the town, just off the A30 to Salisbury, lies Old Wardour Castle, a romantic ruin in a beautiful landscaped setting. The castle had a unique formation, with a pair of square towers sitting at the entrance and an elegant hexagonal shaped courtyard in the middle. It was started in 1392 as a grand mansion rather than for defence, but was twice besieged during the Civil War, first by Parliamentarians and later by Royalists, and both armies caused such damage that the castle was abandoned. In 1769 New Wardour Castle, a Palladian mansion, was built about 1 mile (1.6km) away.

■ Visit

WINCHESTER CHRISTMAS MARKET
Winchester's Christmas market has become a highlight of the city's calendar, with dozens of Scandinavian-style chalets selling high-quality Christmas gifts. The market takes place in the historic cathedral close where choristers rub shoulders with members of the public on the ice rink and the smell of mulled wine and mince pies fills the air.

■ Insight

FISHING THE TEST
The River Test is famous throughout the world for its trout fishing, which has now become one of the most exclusive leisure pursuits in the country. Fishing above and below Stockbridge town is controlled by two famous – and expensive – clubs, which were founded in the early 19th century and now have waiting lists for its membership. The Leckford Club fishes above the village and the prestigious Houghton Club fishes the 10-mile (16km) stretch below the Leckford water.

The city's prestige began to dwindle once the Treasury moved to London, but the aura of past greatness still lingers and it has been said that Winchester's fine High Street has 'a greater wealth of historical associations than any other street in England'. Here you will find the glorious Buttercross, the Guildhall of 1713 (now a bank) with its overhanging City Clock, the arcaded, timbered row known as the Pentice, and the imposing 14th-century Westgate, a small fortified gateway that once served as a debtors' prison. Explore the little alleyways off here for a feel of the old medieval city – Abbey Passage, just below the Victorian Guildhall, is one of the best.

Winchester Castle, where both kings Henry III and Henry VIII's elder brother, Arthur, were born, was destroyed during the Civil War and only the Great Hall remains. The great round table-top which hangs on the west wall has been linked to King Arthur, but was probably made in Tudor times.

The mighty cathedral does not dominate the city, but sits long and low among the trees and lawns of its lovely close. The present solid, squat Norman building was begun in 1097 by Bishop Wakelin on a floating foundation of logs, for the site was half swamp. In the 14th century Bishop William of Wykeham transformed it into what we see today, replacing the flat roof with great ribs and detailed mouldings, adding tall clustered columns around the original piers, and he introduced vast, spacious, elegant fan vaulting. The cathedral is dedicated to St Swithun (died AD 862), who was bishop here, and his tomb lies in the cathedral.

Also here is the tomb of William II (Rufus) and a plain slab to the novelist, Jane Austen, who died near by in College Street in 1817. Look out for delights such as the richly patterned medieval floor tiles, and a stained-glass window in memory of Izaak Walton, the famous angler. During school term time, evensong is sung by the cathedral choir at 5.30pm, Monday to Saturday, and 3.30pm Sunday. Parts of the cathedral doubled as the Vatican for the 2006 blockbuster movie, *The Da Vinci Code*.

The cathedral close contains part of the priory destroyed by Henry VIII's officers, and the City Museum, while near by lie the ruins of the enormous Bishops' Palace, Wolvesey, largely demolished in 1800. The buildings of Winchester College, England's oldest public school, founded in 1387, lie at the end of College Street, and may be toured. A mile away to the south, and overlooking the River Itchen, you'll find the beautiful Hospital of St Cross – fine almshouses that date from the 12th century, with a fine Norman church and an ancient tradition of providing beer and bread for wayfarers, still given today on request from the porter's lodge.

Winchester is not all history, but is a living city, with excellent shopping, many good museums including a restored water mill, and a lively arts scene.

South of Winchester, Marwell Zoo is a family favourite, with lemurs, monkeys, giraffes, penguins, tigers and more. Free road trains make getting around the vast 100-acre (40.5ha) park easy, and there are animal shows and 'meet the keeper' sessions in summer.

■ TOURIST INFORMATION CENTRES

Romsey
Heritage and Visitor Centre,
Church Street.
Tel: 01794 512987

Salisbury
Fish Row.
Tel: 01722 334956;
www.visitsalisbury.com

Shaftesbury
8 Bell Street.
Tel: 01747 853514;
www.shaftesburydorset.com

Winchester
The Guildhall, High Street.
Tel: 01962 840500;
www.visitwinchester.co.uk

■ PLACES OF INTEREST

Avington Park
Winchester.
Tel: 01962 779260;
www.avingtonpark.co.uk

Broadlands
Romsey.
Tel: 01794 505010;
www.broadlands.net

Farley Mount Country Park
West of Winchester.
Tel: 01962 860948;
www.hants.gov.uk/countryside

The Grange (EH)
Northington, near Alresford.
Tel: 01424 775705
Free.

Sir Harold Hillier Gardens
Jermyns Lane, Ampfield, by
Romsey.
Tel: 01794 369318;
www.hilliergardens.org.uk

Hospital of St Cross
St Cross Road, Winchester.
Tel: 01962 851375;
www.stcrosshospital.co.uk

King John's House & Tudor Cottage
Church Street, Romsey.
Tel: 01794 512200;
www.romseyheritage.org.uk

Mompesson House (NT)
Cathedral Close, Salisbury.
Tel: 01722 335659

Mottisfont Abbey Garden (NT)
Near Romsey.
Tel: 01794 340757

Museum of Army Flying
Middle Wallop, Stockbridge.
Tel: 01264 784421;
www.flying-museum.org.uk

Old Sarum (EH)
Castle Road, Salisbury.
Tel: 01722 335398

Old Wardour Castle (EH)
Southwest of Tisbury,
Shaftesbury.
Tel: 01747 870487

Redcoats Military Museum
The Wardrobe, Cathedral
Close, Salisbury.
Tel: 01722 419419;
www.thewardrobe.org.uk

Romsey Abbey
Church Place, Romsey.
Tel: 01794 513125

Salisbury & South Wiltshire Museum
The King's House,
65 The Close, Salisbury.
Tel: 01722 332151;
www.salisburymuseum.org.uk

Salisbury Cathedral
Cathedral Close.
Tel: 01722 555120;
www.salisburycathedral.org.uk

Shaftesbury Abbey Museum & Garden
Park Walk, Shaftesbury.
Tel: 01747 852910; www.
shaftesburyabbey.org.uk

Shaftesbury Town Museum & Garden
Gold Hill.
Tel: 01747 852157

The Watercress Line
The Railway Station,
Station Road, Alresford.
Tel: 01962 733810;
www.watercressline.co.uk

Wilton House
Wilton, Salisbury.
Tel: 01722 746714;
www.wiltonhouse.com

Winchester Castle & Great Hall
Castle Avenue.
Tel: 01962 846476

Winchester Cathedral
The Close.
Tel: 01962 857200;
www.winchester-cathedral.org.uk

Winchester City Mill (NT)
Bridge Street, Winchester.
Tel: 01962 870057

Winchester City Museum
The Square, Winchester.
Tel: 01962 863064;
www.winchester.gov.uk

Winchester College tours
College Street, Winchester.
Tel: 01962 621209

■ FOR CHILDREN

Intech Centre & Planetarium
Telegraph Way, Morn Hill.
Tel: 01962 863791;
www.intech-uk.com

Marwell Wildlife Park
Colden Common, Winchester.
Tel: 01962 777407;
www.marwell.org.uk
Family-friendly zoo.

■ SHOPPING

Broughton Crafts Ltd
High Street, Stockbridge.
Tel: 01264 810513

Cadogan & James
31A The Square, Winchester.
Tel: 01962 840805; www.
cadoganandcompany.co.uk
Superb delicatessen.

Fisherton Mill
108 Fisherton Street,
Salisbury.
Tel: 01722 415121;
www.fishertonmill.co.uk
Contemporary art, furniture
and sculpture.

Justice
80 Parchment Street,
Winchester. Tel: 01962
850890; www.justice.co.uk
Designer jewellery.

Salisbury
Market Tue and Sat; Farmers'
Markets alternate Weds.

Shaftesbury
Market day, every Thu.

■ PERFORMING ARTS

Chesil Theatre
Chesil Street, Winchester.
Tel: 01962 867086;
www.chesiltheatre.org.uk

Salisbury Playhouse
Malthouse Lane, Salisbury.
Tel: 01722 320333;
www.salisburyplayhouse.com

Theatre Royal
21–23 Jewry Street,
Winchester.
Tel: 01962 840440;
www.theatre-royal-
winchester.co.uk

■ SPORTS & ACTIVITIES

CYCLE HIRE
Hayball Cyclesport
The Black Horse Chequer,
26–30 Winchester Street,
Salisbury.
Tel: 01722 411378;
www.hayball.co.uk

FISHING
Avington Trout Fishery
Avington Estate, Avington.
Tel: 01962 779312;
www.avingtontrout.com

Broadlands Estate
Broadlands, Romsey.
Tel: 01794 505010;
www.broadlands.net

RIDING
Grovely Riding Centre
Water Ditchampton, Wilton,
Salisbury.
Tel: 01722 742288;
www.grovely.info

WALKING
Itchen Way
A 25-mile (40.2km) walk
along the River Itchen from
Cheriton to Southampton.

Test Way
A 44-mile (71km) hike from
Inkpen Beacon to Eling
Wharf.

Clarendon Way
A 26-mile (42km) trail from
Winchester to Salisbury.

Avon Valley Path
A 34-mile (55km) route from
Salisbury to Christchurch.

■ ANNUAL EVENTS & CUSTOMS

Alresford
Watercress Festival,
mid-May.

Romsey
Hampshire County Show,
Broadlands Park, end May.
Tel: 01283 820548;
www.livingheritagecountry
shows.co.uk
Romsey Show, Broadlands
Park, early Sep.
Tel: 01794 517521;
www.romseyshow.co.uk

Salisbury
St George's Day. Street
theatre, pageantry and
dragons, 23 Apr.
International Arts Festival.
A variety of art related events
to suit all ages, mid-May to
mid-Jun.
www.salisburyfestival.co.uk

Shaftesbury
Gold Hill Fair, with stalls,
music and dancing. Early Jul.

Winchester
Hat Fair, celebration of street
theatre, late Jun–early Jul.

Tea Rooms

Lillie Langtry's
**High Street, Stockbridge
SO20 6HF
Tel: 01264 810754**

This old building on the main street was once an inn frequented by actress Lillie Langtry. Today it is a homely tea room, serving crumpets dripping with butter and home-made jam, and scones with clotted cream from a neighbouring Jersey herd. You can also enjoy a light lunch here on the shady terrace by the stream.

Grosvenor Hotel
**High Street, Stockbridge
SO20 6EU
Tel: 01264 810606**

Enjoy a cream tea, or toasted tea cakes with a choice of different teas and coffees, in the comfort of this grand old fishing hotel, which juts into the High Street.

Miss Moody's Tea Rooms
**King John's House, Church Street, Romsey SO51 8BT
Tel: 01794 512200**

With its home-made coffee cake, fresh flowers on the tables, friendly service and mismatched floral china teacups, this is surely what a country tea room should be like! Miss Mabel Moody ran a tea room from here in the 1930s, and the tradition continues, with cream teas in summer and light snacks for lunch. There's a pretty courtyard to sit in, too.

Tiffin Tea Rooms
**50 West Street, Alresford
SO24 9AU
Tel: 01962 734394**

This friendly, traditional tea room with its blue-and-white striped awning serves home-made cakes, cream teas and speciality teas and coffees.

Pubs

The Haunch of Venison
**1–5 Minster Street, Salisbury
SP1 1TB
Tel: 01722 411313**

Craftsmen working on the cathedral spire were some of the early customers of this pub, dating back to 1320. A restaurant in summer serves treats such as pork with coriander and ginger and coconut Thai nage. Beers include Courage Best.

The Mayfly
**Testcombe, Stockbridge
SO20 6AZ
Tel: 01264 860283**

A lovely old country pub, the Mayfly looks onto the fast-flowing River Test. A selection of hot and cold meats, quiches and pies is laid out buffet-style, along with a few hot daily specials. Beers include Ringwood Best and Wadworth 6X.

The Plough Inn
**Main Road, Sparsholt
SO21 2NW
Tel: 01962 776353**

Originally the coach house for Sparsholt Manor, the Plough has been tastefully extended over the years and offers a harmonious interior decorated with old farming tools, stone jars and dried hops to complement the real ales and good food on offer. One end of the bar offers light meals such as Thai green curry and mushroom tagliatelle, while the far end offers more substantial dishes fare, such as braised lamb shank.

The Wykeham Arms
**75 Kingsgate Street, Winchester SO23 9PE
Tel: 01962 853834**

The 'Wyk', in an old back street near to Winchester College, is a local institution. It is furnished in part with old desks and ephemera from the school. The food is excellent, ranging from the Wyk cottage pie, to rack of lamb and duck breast. There is a choice of around 20 wines by the glass, and 60 more by the bottle.

TOURIST INFORMATION CENTRES

Bournemouth
Westover Road.
Tel: 0845 051 1700;
www.bournemouth.co.uk

Lyndhurst
New Forest Visitor
Information Centre,
Main car park.
Tel: 023 8028 2269;
www.thenewforest.co.uk

Newport
The Guildhall, High Street.
Tel: 01983 813818

Portsmouth
Clarence Esplanade,
Southsea.
Tel: 023 9282 6722

Winchester
The Guildhall, High Street.
Tel: 01962 840500;
www.visitwinchester.co.uk

OTHER INFORMATION

New Forest Ranger Service
Forestry Commission, The
Queen's House, Lyndhurst.
Tel: 023 8028 6840;
www.forestry.gov.uk/
newforest

The National Trust (NT)
PO Box 39, Warrington WA5
7WD. Tel: 0870 458 4000;
www.nationaltrust.org.uk

English Heritage (EH)
PO Box 569
Swindon SN2 2YP.
Tel: 0870 333 1181;
www.english-heritage.org.uk

English Nature (EN)
(Hampshire and Isle of Wight

Team) 1 Southampton Road,
Lyndhurst, Hampshire
SO43 7BU.
Tel: 023 8028 6410;
www.english-nature.org.uk

**Royal Society for the
Protection of Birds (RSPB)**
The Lodge, Sandy,
Bedfordshire SG19 2DL.
Tel: 01767 680551;
www.rspb.org.uk

Beaches
Lifeguards are generally
found on busy beaches during
the summer season. Dogs
may not be allowed on some
beaches during busy summer
months.

Coastguard
For Coastguard Assistance
dial 999 and ask for the
Coastguard Service, which
co-ordinates rescue services.

Parking
Information on parking
permits and car parks in the
area is available from local
Tourist Information Centres
and on the Web.

Places of Interest
There will be an admission
charge unless stated. For
further information about
specific places or attractions
contact the relevant local TIC
or check on the internet.

Weather
www.onlineweather.com

**PUBLIC TRANSPORT
Traveline**
Tel: 0871 200 2233;
www.traveline.org.uk

Red Funnel Ferries
Town Quay, Southampton.
Tel: 0870 444 8898;
www.redfunnel.co.uk

Wight Link Ferries
Tel: 0870 582 774
Hythe Ferry.
Tel: 02380 840722;
www.hytheferry.co.uk

Gosport Ferry
Tel: 023 9252 4551;
www.gosportferry.co.uk

Hovertravel
Clarence Esplanade,
Southsea.
Tel: 02392 811000;
www.hovertravel.co.uk

ORDNANCE SURVEY MAPS

EAST DORSET
Explorer Outdoor Leisure
1:25,000; Sheet 15

NEW FOREST
Explorer Outdoor Leisure
1:25,000; Sheets 22 and 130

ISLE OF WIGHT
Explorer Outdoor Leisure
1:25,000; Sheet 29

**PORTSMOUTH & SOUTH
EAST COAST**
Explorer Outdoor Leisure
1:25,000; Sheets 22 and 119

WINCHESTER & SALISBURY
Explorer Outdoor Leisure
1:25,000; Sheets 130 and 132

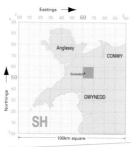

The National Grid system covers Great Britain with an imaginary network of grid squares. Each is 100km square in area and is given a unique alphabetic reference, as shown in the diagram above.

These squares are sub-divided into one hundred 10km squares, identified by vertical lines (eastings) and horizontal lines (northings). The reference for the square a feature is located within is made by adding the numbers of the two lines which cross the bottom left corner of that square to the alphabetic reference (ignoring the small figures). The easting is quoted first. For example, SH6050.

For a 2-figure reference, the zeros are omitted, giving just SH65. In this book, we use 4-figure references, which allow us to pinpoint the feature more accurately by dividing the 10km square into one hundred 1km squares. These squares are not actually printed on the road atlas but are estimated by eye. The same process is carried out as before, giving an enhanced reference of SH6154.

Key to Atlas

M4	Motorway with number
S	Motorway service area — Fleet
	Motorway toll
	Motorway junction with and without number
3	Restricted motorway junctions
	Motorway and junction under construction
A3	Primary route single/dual carriageway
BATH	Primary route destinations
	Roundabout
5	Distance in miles between symbols
A1123	Other A Road single/dual carriageway
B2070	B road single/dual carriageway
	Unclassified road single/dual carriageway
⊨=====⊣	Road tunnel

Toll	Toll
	Road underconstruction
	Narrow Primary route with passing places
→	Steep gradient
—○—✕—	Railway station and level crossing
+++++++++	Tourist railway
― ― ― ―	National trail
....	Forest drive
⌣⌣⌣	Heritage coast
⟷	Ferry route
6	Walk start point
1	Cycle start point
3	Tour start point

⛪	Abbey, cathedral or priory
🐠	Aquarium
⚔	Castle
⌒	Cave
❦	Country park
🏏	County cricket ground
	Farm or animal centre
❋	Garden
⚑	Golf course
🏠	Historic house
	Horse racing
	Motor racing
🏛	Museum
⊕	Airport
Ⓗ	Heliport
🗼	Windmill
NT	National Trust property

NTS	National Trust for Scotland property
	Nature reserve
★	Other place of interest
P·R	Park and Ride location
⚲	Picnic site
	Steam centre
	Ski slope natural
	Ski slope artifical
🅙	Tourist Information Centre
	Viewpoint
🄿	Visitor or heritage centre
	Zoological or wildlife collection
	Forest Park
	National Park (England & Wales)
	National Scenic Area (Scotland)

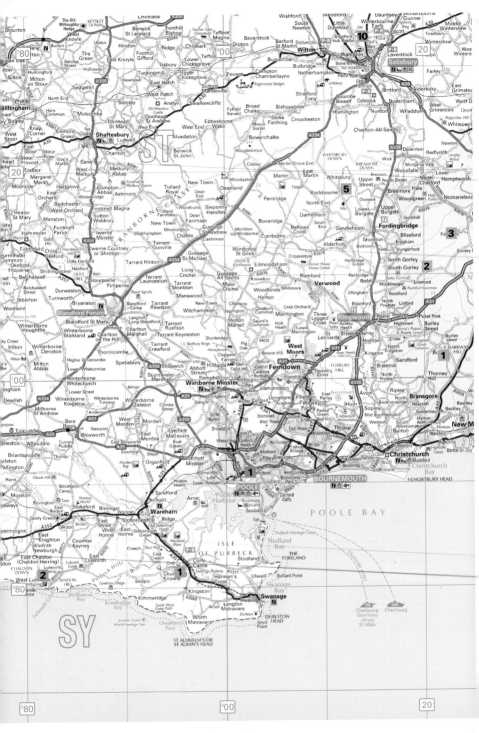

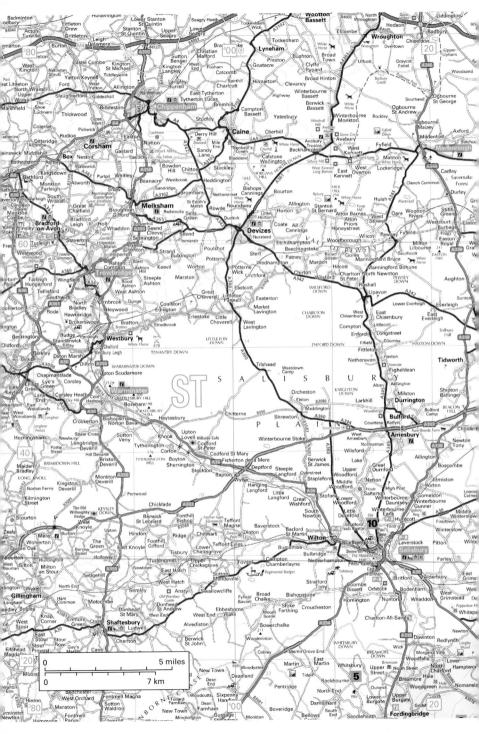

The Automobile Association wishes to thank the following photographers and organisations for their assistance in the preparation of this book.

Abbreviations for the picture credits are as follows – (t) top; (b) bottom; (l) left; (r) right; (c) centre; (AA) AA World Travel Library

1 AA/Adam Burton; 4–5 AA/Adam Burton; 7 AA/Adam Burton; 8t AA/Max Jourdan; 8bl AA/Adam Burton; 8cr AA/Adam Burton; 8br AA/Adam Burton; 9 AA/Simon McBride; 10t AA/Adam Burton; 10c AA/Adam Burton; 10b AA/Adam Burton; 11t AA/Adam Burton; 11b AA/Wyn Voysey; 13 AA/Adam Burton; 14 AA/Steve Day; 18 AA/Adam Burton; 21tl AA/Adam Burton; 21tr AA/Adam Burton; 21cr AA/Richard Ireland; 21b AA/Adam Burton; 22cl AA/Adam Burton; 22cr AA/Adam Burton; 22b AA/Max Jourdan; 23t AA/Philip Enticknap; 23c AA/James Tims; 23b AA/Adam Burton; 28 AA/James Tims; 35 AA/Adam Burton; 40 AA/Adam Burton; 46 AA/Adam Burton; 48 AA/A J Hopkins; 51t AA/Adam Burton; 51bl AA/Wyn Voysey; 51br AA/Adam Burton; 52cl AA/Adam Burton; 52cr AA/Adam Burton; 52b AA/Adam Burton; 53t AA/Adam Burton; 53c AA/Adam Burton; 53b AA/Adam Burton; 56 AA/Derek Forss; 61 AA/Adam Burton; 68 AA/Adam Burton; 74/75 AA/Adam Burton; 80 AA/Adam Burton; 82 AA/Adam Burton; 85tl AA/Adam Burton; 85tr AA/Adam Burton; 85br AA/Adam Burton; 86c AA/Adam Burton; 86b AA/Adam Burton; 87t AA/Adam Burton; 87c AA/Adam Burton; 87b AA/Adam Burton; 90 AA/Adam Burton; 98 AA/Adam Burton; 104 AA/Simon McBride; 106 AA/Adam Burton; 109t AA/Wyn Voysey; 109b AA/Wyn Voysey; 110 AA/Adam Burton; 111t AA/Derek Croucher; 111b AA/Adam Burton; 124 AA/Derek Croucher; 126 AA/James Tims; 128 AA/Michael Moody; 129t AA/Adam Burton; 129b AA/James Tims; 130l AA/James Tims; 130cr AA/Michael Moody; 130br AA/James Tims; 131t AA/Michael Moody; 131b AA/Michael Moody; 139 AA/James Tims; 146 AA/Michael Moody; 150 AA/James Tims.

Every effort has been made to trace the copyright holders, and we apologise in advance for any accidental errors. We would be happy to apply any corrections in the following edition of this publication.